His Story, Our Response

What The Bible Says About
SUBJECTS YOU CARE ABOUT

His Story — Our Response: What the Bible Says about Worship
Dinelle Frankland

Listening to His Heartbeat: What the Bible Says about the Heart of God
Harold Shank

Power from On High: What the Bible Says about the Holy Spirit
Jack Cottrell

Where Is God When We Suffer? What the Bible Says about Suffering
Lynn Gardner

Other Topics in the Planning:
The Afterlife, The Church, The Doctrine of God, Grace (coming soon from Cottrell), Prayer

What The Bible Says About

WORSHIP

His Story, Our Response

Dinelle Frankland

COLLEGE PRESS PUBLISHING COMPANY · JOPLIN, MISSOURI

Copyright © 2008
2nd Printing, 2009
College Press Publishing Co
Since 1959, publishers of resources for preachers, teachers,
and Bible students
Order toll-free 800-289-3300
On the web at WWW.COLLEGEPRESS.COM
Publishers also of HeartSpring Books

International Standard Book Number: 978-0-89900-963-6

Common Abbreviations
Used in this Series

AD .... *Anno Domini*
ASV .... American Standard Version
BC .... Before Christ
KJV .... King James Version
LXX .... *Septuagint*
MT .... Masoretic Text
NASB .... New American Standard Bible
NIV .... New International Version
NT .... New Testament
OT .... Old Testament
RSV .... Revised Standard Version

ABOUT THE SERIES

"What does the Bible say about that?" This is a question that should concern every Bible-believing Christian, whatever the particular subject being discussed. Granted, we know there are situations and activities that are not directly addressed by the Bible, because of changes in society, culture, and technology. However, if we truly believe that the Bible is to be our guide for living and especially for developing our relationship with God, then we need to look to it for information that will impact our everyday decisions. Even what may seem like abstract doctrinal matters will affect our religious practices, and if the Bible is indeterminate on a particular issue, then we need to know that too, so that we don't waste time on the kinds of controversies Paul warns about in 1 Timothy 1:4.

College Press Publishing Company is fully committed to equipping our customers as Bible students. In addition to commentary series and small study books on individual books of the Bible, this is not the first time we have done a series of books specifically dedicated to this question: "What DOES the Bible say?" Part of this stems from the background of CPPC as a publishing house of what has generally been known as the "Restoration Movement,"[1] a movement that

---

[1] In order to be more specific and recognize that these churches are not necessarily unique in the plea to restore the church of the apostles, it is also known as the "Stone-Campbell Movement," after the names of some of the 19th-century leaders of the movement.

gave rise to Churches of Christ and Christian Churches. The "restoration" of the movement's name refers to the desire to restore biblical teaching and emphases to our religious beliefs and activities.

It is important to understand what this series can and cannot do. Every author in the series will be passing the exact words of the biblical text through a filter of his or her own best understanding of the implications of those words. Nor will the Bible be the only source to be quoted. Various human authors will inevitably be referenced either in support of the conclusions reached or to contradict their teachings. Keeping this in mind, you should use them as tools to direct your own study of the Bible, and use the "Berean principle" of studying carefully every part of the Bible to see "whether these things [are] so" (Acts 17:11, ASV). We would not be true to our own purpose if we encouraged you to take any book that we publish as the "last word" on any subject. Our plea, our desire, is to make "every Christian a Bible Student."

A WORD ABOUT FORMAT

In order to emphasize the theme of "What the Bible Says," we have chosen to place Scripture quotations and Scripture references in distinct typestyles to make them stand out. Use of these typestyles within quotations of other works should not be taken as an indication that the original author similarly emphasized the highlighted text.

"Fear God and give him glory,
because the hour of his judgment has come.
Worship him who made
the heavens, the earth,
the sea and the springs of water."

Revelation 14:7

PREFACE

It is both overwhelming and humbling to write "What the Bible Says" about *anything*. Worship, however, has been a passion of mine for many years now, and it is my hope that I can in some small way offer assistance to others who may have the same desire to see it accomplished in a biblical way. This may not be the most definitive work, but I am hopeful that it will spark interest for continued reflection and study.

I am grateful to three friends who gave me encouragement toward this task: Mark Moore, who believed that I could write it; Brian Lowery, who did not laugh when I first shared my ideas; and Sue Jones, who gave me regular pep talks. I am deeply indebted to Julie Yarwood, who edited, checked sources, and helped me clarify my thoughts, and to Miriam Windham, Josh Weber, Gary Hall, and Neal Windham, who read the book and gave me invaluable insights and corrections. Of course, no endeavor such as this would be possible without the input of many fine teachers; I especially wish to acknowledge Rick Terry, Bruce Leafblad, and the late Robert E. Webber, all of whom changed the course of my life in some way that brought me to this point. Additionally, I am thankful to a group of students from Ozark Christian College who shared in my doctoral work, and thus in the completion of this endeavor.

This book is dedicated to Grant, Keller, Grace, and Lily, who fill my life with much more than great illustrations.

[3] Great and marvelous are your deeds,
Lord God Almighty.
Just and true are your ways,
King of the ages.
[4] Who will not fear you, O Lord,
and bring glory to your name?
For you alone are holy.
All nations will come
and worship before you,
for your righteous acts have been revealed.
Revelation 15:3-4

IN THIS BOOK

Forgiveness

God's salvation plan brought the world from darkness to light. Worship is impacted by the recognition of sin and death, as Christians celebrate being freed by the once-and-for-all sacrifice of Jesus.

Baffled by Mystery

Biblical worship is lifestyle worship. The Holy Spirit enables living a life worthy of God and empowers vital corporate gatherings.

INTRODUCTION

T"ell me a story, Aunt Dinelle," are words I have heard repeatedly since the time my oldest nephew could talk. Passed down to his brother and sisters, the hunger for stories continues and is almost certainly a part of any visit to their home. These stories, generally made up on the spur of the moment, are neither literary masterpieces nor particularly clever. They are usually quite fanciful, however, and always include the escapades of my nieces and nephews. Even when we grow up, we never seem to lose the desire to hear a good story.

A biblical study reveals that worship involves, at its roots and heart, a story. Far from being distant and irrelevant, this story gives us reason to rejoice, to praise, to hope, to give, to belong, to lament, and most importantly, to respond.

> Because it is God who always takes the initiative, Christian worship is best discussed in the terms of *response*. In worship we respond to God and this is true of the whole of liturgy, whether it be praise, thanksgiving, supplication, or repentance, whether it be Eucharist or baptism, or liturgical prayer or the celebration of the Church's year. If this is so, worship must be seen in the context of saving history, which is the record of the divine initiative. **(Crichton, 9)**

I have chosen to consider our response to certain attributes of God. The possi-

A biblical study reveals that worship involves, at its roots and heart, a story.

bilities, of course, are infinite, but these particular pictures of the Divine evoke certain responses in Scripture that give us something concrete to consider.

The story of worship begins with creation. It winds its way through God's redemptive plan and the incredible gift of forgiveness. At the center stands Jesus Christ, the One and Only, who makes worship in spirit and truth possible. This story is still being written, and will not culminate until we stand before the Throne "lost in wonder, love and praise."[1] Our part of the story includes confession and repentance, offering and thanksgiving, praise and remembering, belonging and serving, all prompted by the work of the Holy Spirit.

This book is a journey through this story. It is an attempt to offer a study, primarily of corporate worship, viewed through the lens of biblical history.

There is no attempt in the following pages to "define" worship, because in Scripture worship is not so much

In Scripture worship is not so much defined as described.

defined as described. Throughout history God's people have worshiped, both when gathered and scattered, corporately and privately, in a myriad of ways.

I believe in "whole-life worship," and would prefer another term to describe what we do when we gather on Sunday morning. A good choice is the word "liturgy," but many in the Christian Church distrust the word. Derived from the Greek, *leitourgia*, which means "service" or "work of the people," liturgy simply denotes what we do as the gathered people of God.

It is hoped that the reader will recognize that while the biblical principles presented here transcend culture, every body of believers finds itself in its own unique story, and church leaders must do their part in applying these principles to his or her own context.

[1] Charles Wesley, "Love Divine, All Loves Excelling."

⁸Give thanks to the LORD, call on his name;
make known among the nations what he has done.
⁹Sing to him, sing praise to him;
tell of all his wonderful acts.
¹⁰Glory in his holy name;
let the hearts of those who seek the LORD rejoice.
¹¹Look to the LORD and his strength;
seek his face always.
¹²Remember the wonders he has done,
his miracles, and the judgments he pronounced. . . .

²³Sing to the LORD, all the earth;
proclaim his salvation day after day.
²⁴Declare his glory among the nations,
his marvelous deeds among all peoples.
²⁵For great is the LORD and most worthy of praise;
he is to be feared above all gods.
²⁹ . . . ascribe to the Lord the glory due his name.
. . . worship the Lord in the splendor of his holiness.
³⁴Give thanks to the LORD, for he is good;
his love endures forever.
³⁶Praise be to the LORD, the God of Israel,
from everlasting to everlasting.
Then all the people said "Amen" and "Praise the LORD."

1Chr 16:8-12,23-25,29,34,36

Worship

Is

Too Big

for

Us

A few years ago my nephews got a "Twister" game for Christmas. My way of playing the game is to say, "I'll spin; you twist." The fun wore off quickly, and the boys were ready to move on to something else. Wanting to be a good responsible aunt, I insisted that they put the game away first. Being ornery boys, they didn't. My niece, however, who was about two years old, was watching carefully. She walked over to that big plastic sheet, and tried with her tiny little arms to gather it up. Of course it was too big for her, but it seemed that she only wanted to please me. And I loved her so much at that moment.

When we attempt to worship God, whose vastness and superiority are incomprehensible, He knows that the task is too big for us. But much of worship concerns wanting to please Him, and I believe He loves us when we try.

CHAPTER ONE
GOD, THE CREATOR

In the beginning God created the heavens and the earth.
Genesis 1:1

. . . This first chapter of Genesis breathes worship. . . . Its central concern is not to explain the how of creation, but to catch the reader up with the wonder of creation. This is not to exalt the creation itself, but is an invitation to worship the Creator. . . . The Bible never speaks of the doctrine of creation purely out of intellectual curiosity. Creation is used to encourage worship, to increase faith, and to change perspective on our life in the light of the nature of God. **(Wilkinson, 29-30)**

WORSHIP BEGINS WITH CREATION

The story of worship begins with creation. Imagine the lives of Adam and Eve before the Fall. They were constantly in the presence of God, who made the world and everything in it. He produced life out of nothing, light out of darkness, beauty out of formlessness. D.A. Carson deduces, "There was no need to exhort human beings in worship; their entire existence revolved around the God who had made them" **(34)**. The first human response must have been pure, unadulterated worship.

An Old Testament Perspective

Edward Young acknowledges, "Whenever man in seriousness contemplates the heavens he is met with God's handiwork, for the marvelous bodies of heaven point him to the Creator" (61).

> 25 "To whom will you compare me?
>   Or who is my equal?" says the Holy One.
> 26 Lift your eyes and look to the heavens:
>   Who created all these?
> He who brings out the starry host one by one,
>   and calls them each by name.
> Because of his great power and mighty strength,
>   not one of them is missing.
> 27 Why do you say, O Jacob,
>   and complain, O Israel,
> "My way is hidden from the LORD;
>   my cause is disregarded by my God"?
> 28 Do you not know?
>   Have you not heard?
> The LORD is the everlasting God,
>   the Creator of the ends of the earth.
> He will not grow tired or weary,
>   and his understanding no one can fathom.
>
> *(Isa 40:25-28)*

In the above passage and elsewhere in Scripture, God, the Creator, stands against all other gods. The ancient world was full of religions that promoted the worship of all manner of deities, which were often related to nature. The spiritual leaders of Israel, therefore, were routinely contending with the allure of worshiping idols. Jeremiah, for example, deals with the issue of false

The spiritual leaders of Israel were routinely contending with the allure of worshiping idols.

gods by contrasting them with a portrait of the *only* God capable of creation:

> [11]*"Tell them this: 'These gods, who did not make the heavens and the earth, will perish from the earth and from under the heavens.'"*
> [12]*But God made the earth by his power;*
> *he founded the world by his wisdom*
> *and stretched out the heavens by his understanding.*
> [13]*When He thunders, the waters in the heavens roar;*
> *he makes clouds rise from the ends of the earth.*
> *He sends lightning with the rain*
> *and brings out the wind from his storehouses.*
> [14]*Everyone is senseless and without knowledge;*
> *every goldsmith is shamed by his idols.*
> *His images are a fraud;*
> *they have no breath in them.*
> [15]*They are worthless, the objects of mockery;*
> *when their judgment comes, they will perish.*
> [16]*He who is the Portion of Jacob is not like these,*
> *for he is the Maker of all things,*
> *including Israel, the tribe of his inheritance—*
> *the LORD Almighty is his name. (**Jer 10:11-16**)*

Acceptance of this one and only Creator requires worship. Walter Brueggemann notes that "Israel has the option to be in relationship with and loyal to the God who can give new life. This God must be trusted and served and is never at the disposal of Israel" (*Jeremiah*, 105). Of course, the children of Israel often forgot this relationship, worshiping according to their own desires. In fact, the following chapters of Jeremiah deal with the repercussions of the broken covenant.[1]

After the return of the Jews from the Babylonian captivity, Nehemiah led them in both physical (the rebuilding of the city) and spiritual reform. Following an emotional and joyous reading of God's Word, and several hours of confession, the gathered Israelites recognized the sovereignty of God as manifested in His creation:

---

[1] The relationship between covenant and worship will be discussed in chapter 3.

*⁵Blessed be your glorious name, and may it be exalted above all blessing and praise. ⁶You alone are the LORD. You made the heavens, even the highest heavens, and all their starry host, the earth and all that is on it, the seas and all that is in them. You give life to everything, and the multitudes of heaven worship you. (**Neh 9:5b-6**)²*

A NEW TESTAMENT PERSPECTIVE

The acknowledgement of the Creator does not end with the OT.

> The Christological focus of the doctrine of creation in the New Testament can also serve as a reminder that creation is centered on Jesus Christ, the incarnate Logos, and not on the human species. . . . Significant sections of the New Testament develop the Old Testament trajectory of creation traditions and demonstrate a deep continuity with the faith of Israel. **(18)**

In Romans, Paul makes it clear that it is the Creator who is to be worshiped: *They exchanged the truth of God for a lie, and worshiped and served created things rather than the Creator— who is forever praised. Amen* (**Rom 1:25**). In Colossians, the apostle gives Jesus Christ the title, "firstborn over all creation," which gives Him sovereignty over everything:

> *¹⁵He is the image of the invisible God, the firstborn over all creation. ¹⁶For by him all things were created: things in heaven and on earth, visible and invisible, whether thrones or powers or rulers or authorities; all things were created by him and for him. ¹⁷He is before all things, and in him all things hold together* (**Col 1:15-17**).

The Colossians passage sets Jesus Christ squarely at the center of worship. Christ is supreme and infinite. He rules now, and deserves our devotion and praise. He makes this world livable because He died, as Isaac Watts eloquently penned, "for man the creature's sin."³

The Book of Revelation affirms that biblical worship is a

---

²The remainder of this prayer rehearses the deeds of Yahweh, another significant feature of worship which will be discussed in chapter 2.

³"Alas! And Did My Savior Bleed?" Words by Isaac Watts.

response to who God is and what He has done. Carson points to *Revelation 4*, where God is worshiped simply because He is Creator and reigns over us:

Biblical worship is a response to who God is and what He has done.

> *[9]Whenever the living creatures give glory, honor and thanks to him who sits on the throne and who lives for ever and ever, [10]the twenty-four elders fall down before him who sits on the throne, and worship him who lives for ever and ever. They lay their crowns before the throne and say: [11]"You are worthy, our Lord and God, to receive glory and honor and power, **for you created all things, and by your will they were created and have their being.**"* (**Rev 4:9-11**, emphasis added)

Carson continues: "Worship is the proper response of the creature to the Creator. Worship does not create something new; rather, it is a transparent response to what is, a recognition of our creaturely status before the Creator himself" (**28-29**). This seemingly simple truth must not be lost in our attempt to "create worship experiences" for our local church bodies. We simply have no power to do so. The power rests in the Creator God, who has given us hearts and minds that we willingly give over to the prompting of the Holy Spirit.

Marva Dawn suggests that we can learn from the cosmic praise depicted in the marvelous book of Revelation:

> When we look carefully at how the heavens respond to God's reign, we find many hints for how we might worship now in practice for the ultimate fulfillment of God's promises. What can we learn from angels' worship of God? What do they express in their songs, and how might that teach us about true praise? (**Royal Waste**, 365)

The angels insist upon worship as a response to God, the Creator:

> *Then I saw another angel flying in midair, and he had the eternal gospel to proclaim to those who live on the earth—to every nation, tribe, language and people. He said in a loud voice, "Fear God and give him glory, because the hour of his judgment has come. Worship him who made the heavens, the earth, the sea and the springs of water."* (**Rev 14:6-7**)

Apart from acknowledging that God is God and we are not, the perspective of creation should also cause us to consider the diversity with which we respond. Created in His image, we must certainly expect to worship Him with all of the creativity we can muster. David Wilkinson exhorts,

> **Created in His image, we must certainly expect to worship Him with all of the creativity we can muster.**

"Alongside the image of lawgiver, king and logician, the Genesis account gives us the picture of God as the great artist. Here is creativity and diversity in abundance"(27).

Worship gatherings have always contained elements of artistic expression which allow the created to connect in a small way with the vastness and beauty of the Creator. The expressions vary, but all have been derived from the Spirit-empowered imaginations of God's people. Nevertheless, organized religion has struggled for centuries with the seeming dichotomy between art and idolatry, especially pointing to the second commandment: *"You shall not make for yourself an idol in the form of anything in heaven above or on the earth beneath or in the waters below"* (*Ex 20:4*). But it is *idolatry* that is prohibited, not the artistic process. The building of the tabernacle, which was supervised by God, testifies to the appropriate use of creativity in worship, as does the later, more extravagant temple.

> **God has no argument with aesthetic beauty designed to bring Him glory.**

Both verify that God has no argument with aesthetic beauty designed to bring Him glory.

RESPONSE: PRAISE AND THANKSGIVING

OLD TESTAMENT VOCABULARY

An overview of worship vocabulary in the OT reveals multifaceted expressions that portray a response to the Creator.

For example, *shachah*, "the Hebrew word usually translated 'worship' in English means, literally, to bow down" (**R. Leonard, "Vocabulary,"** 3).[4] Ralph Martin explains that the word "emphasizes the way in which an Israelite fittingly thought of his approach to the holy presence of God. He bows himself down in lowly reverence and prostration" (*Early*, 11). This is the action considered to be appropriate in the presence of a leader or king.[5] Andrew Hill assigns an attitude of humility to this expression that is "prompted by the recognition of one's rank or standing in the order of God's creation" (7).

Acknowledging God verbally is seen in Scripture as being a significant part of a believer's worshiping life. A common word, *halal*, is found over 40 times in the Psalms alone.[6] This rich word means "to praise, commend, or be boastful." Also meaning "praise" were *tehillah* (*Pss 22:3,25; 33:1; 34:1*), *yadah*, which generally means to confess the name of God, or give thanks (*Gen 29:35; 1Kgs 8:33; 1Chr 16:4,7,8,34,35; Pss 9:1; 32:5; 35:18*), and *todah*, a noun generally translated "thanksgiving" (*Pss 69:30; 95:2; 100:4; Neh 12:27; Jer 17:26*). Also of note are *shabah*, "to laud, commend, or congratulate" (*Pss 63:3; 106:47*), *yarum*, "to exalt" (*Pss 18:46; 34:3*), and *gadal*, "to magnify" (*Ps 34:3; 1Chr 17:24*).

Musical offerings occur

> **Acknowledging God verbally is seen in Scripture as being a significant part of a believer's worshiping life.**

with regularity in the praise of Yahweh as well. The word, *ranan* (*1Chr 16:33; Pss 33:1; 51:14; 67:4; 81:1; Isa 44:23; Jer 31:7*), is translated as "sing," "rejoice" or "give a ringing cry." *Psalm 101:1*, *"I will sing of your love and justice; to you, O LORD, I will*

---

[4] For a comprehensive and concise treatment of OT vocabulary, this source is recommended.

[5] *Gen 27:29*: *"May nations serve you and peoples bow down to you."* *1Sa 25:23*: *"When Abigail saw David, she quickly got off her donkey and bowed down before David with her face to the ground."* *2Sa 14:33*: *"Then the king summoned Absalom, and he came in and bowed down with his face to the ground before the king."*

[6] See *Pss 18:3; 22:22; 44:8; 56:10; 96:4; 104:35; 113:1, etc.* The Chronicles also abound with this word: *1Chr 16:4,10,25,36; 23:5,30*, for example.

sing praise," yields two Hebrew words for singing, *shiyr*[7] and *zamar*.[8] The latter sees musical instruments being used in biblical worship. Jubal is recognized as *"the father of all who play the harp and flute"* (**Gen 4:21**). Most references to instruments are found during and following the time of David. These include harps, lyres, tambourines, cymbals, sistrums, and trumpets.[9]

Along with verbal praise, response to God as seen in the OT consistently involves posture. For example, *kara'*, meaning "to bend, kneel, bow, bow down, sink down to one's knees, kneel in reverence" (**2Chr 7:3; Isa 45:23**); *barak*, meaning "to bend the knee," but most often translated, "bless," (**Ps 95:6**);[10] *qûm*, to "stand" or "rise up" (**Pss 24:3; 119:62; Isa 49:7**); *'amad*, "stand" (**Neh 8:5; Ps 134:1**); and *nasa'*, "lift up" the hands (**Ps 63:4**), heads (**Ps 24:9**), or souls (**Ps 25:1**), are a few such expressions.

> **Response to God as seen in the OT consistently involves posture.**

Clearly there was physicality about the celebrations of the OT. Dance (*machowl*), for example, was not uncommon (**Pss 30:11; 149:3; 150:4**). When David brought the Ark of the Covenant to Jerusalem, he was leaping and dancing (**2Sa 6:16**).[11] **Psalm 47:1** commands God's followers to clap and shout.[12]

Such physical responses, says David Peterson, were "the culturally accepted way of responding to great ones and benefactors in the ancient world" (**63**). They were adopted and became "a means of acknowledging the power and grace

---

[7] See also **Ex 15:1,21; 1Chr 16:9,23; Ps 33:3**.
[8] See also **Jdg 5:3; 2Sa 22:50; Ps 33:2**.
[9] **1Chr 13:8; 15:16; 16:42; 23:5; 2Sa 6:5; Neh 12:36; Pss 33:2; 71:22; 150:3-5; Isa 38:20**. See also the headings of **Pss 4, 6, 54, 55, 61, 67, 76**.
[10] See also **1Chr 16:36; 29:10; Pss 26:12; 41:13; 103:1,2,20,21,22; Neh 9:5**. It is used with frequency. While it is commonly used in relationship to God's people blessing Him, God may also bless His people (**Ps 67:1,6,7**).
[11] *Pazaz*, "to bound, be agile," and *karar*, "to whirl or dance."
[12] *Taqa'* sometimes translated "to blow" or "give a blast" and *ruwa'* often used in battle; see **1Sa 17:52; 2Chr 13:15**. Sometimes translated "make a joyful noise."

of God" (ibid.). But to take these physical responses at face value and insist that we adapt them to our modern-day gatherings would deny their intent, which is genuine reverence and awe in the presence of the Creator. Forcing or manipulating responses of any kind is foreign to worship as seen in Scripture. Instead of doing so, we should present God in the best way we can and get out of the way. Oswald Chambers wrote, "Worship is giving God the best that He has given you" (*Utmost*, January 6).

We see also that God was not pleased with outward expressions alone. This nuance is suggested when God enlists Moses to bring His people out of Egypt, promising

> "Worship is giving God the best that He has given you."

"you will worship God on this mountain" (*Ex 3:12*). The word translated "worship" here, *'abad*, means "work" or "service."[13] Putting Yahweh at the center of life, publicly and privately, requires wholehearted devotion which manifests itself in acts of service.

Not all of Israel's praise was boisterous and physical. *Psalm 65:1* states, *"Praise awaits you, O God, in Zion; to you our vows will be fulfilled."* The Hebrew word translated "awaits" is *dûmiyah*, which indicates silence of repose. In the midst of *Psalm 46*, a declaration of God's strength and help in troubled times, God himself reminds the worshiper to *"be still and know that I am God."*[14] The intent of the word here is to "let drop," or "relax." In other words, the stillness of this verse is generated by a deep and abiding trust in God, who promises that He is in control and will protect His children from calamity.

Habakkuk's command for the whole world to be silent[15] is brought about by the presence of God, who is *"in His holy*

---

[13] This word is prominent when God demands that the Israelites be released from bondage in Egypt, as we shall see in chapter 2. See also *Num 4:26,37,41; Deu 11:13,16; Josh 24:15; Pss 2:11; 100:2*.

[14] *Ps 46:10*. The Hebrew word is *rapah*.

[15] *Hasah*, "hush, be silent, hold the tongue." See also *Zep 1:7* and *Zec 2:13*.

temple" (**Hab 2:20**). Whether this refers to the temple in Jerusalem or more generically to the heavenly temple, the point is the same. There is reason to cease all activity with reverence and awe in the presence of the Almighty. Unlike the dead gods of Babylon that the prophet rails against (**Hab 2:18-19**), Yahweh is ruler of all, and listens and responds to His people. Worshiping one's own creation is futile.

THE ENTRANCE PSALMS: WHO MAY ENTER THE PRESENCE OF GOD?

Psalms 15 and 24, known as the Entrance Psalms, "invite theological reflection on what it means to enter God's reign and to submit to God's sovereign claim upon the life of God's people and the world," maintains J. Clinton McCann (**Book, 651**). When coming before God, concludes Ronald Manahan, "Worshipers ought to sense their separation from God; they are His guests" (**69**).

> ¹LORD, who may dwell in your sanctuary?
>   Who may live on your holy hill?
> ²He whose walk is blameless
>   and who does what is righteous,
> who speaks the truth from his heart
>   ³and has no slander on his tongue,
> who does his neighbor no wrong
>   and casts no slur on his fellowman,
> ⁴who despises a vile man
>   but honors those who fear the LORD,
> who keeps his oath
>   even when it hurts,
> ⁵who lends his money without usury
>   and does not accept a bribe against the innocent.
> He who does these things
>   will never be shaken. (**Psalm 15**)
>
> ¹The earth is the LORD's, and everything in it,
>   the world, and all who live in it;
> ²for he founded it upon the seas
>   and established it upon the waters
> ³Who may ascend the hill of the LORD?

Who may stand in his holy place?
⁴He who has clean hands and a pure heart,
    who does not lift up his soul to an idol
    or swear by what is false.
⁵He will receive blessing from the LORD
    and vindication from God his Savior.
⁶Such is the generation of those who seek him,
    who seek your face, O God of Jacob.
⁷Lift up your heads, O you gates;
    be lifted up, you ancient doors,
    that the King of glory may come in.
⁸Who is this King of glory?
    The LORD strong and mighty,
    the LORD mighty in battle.
⁹Lift up your heads, O you gates;
    lift them up, you ancient doors,
    that the King of glory may come in.
¹⁰Who is he, this King of glory?
    The LORD Almighty—
    he is the King of glory. (**Psalm 24**)

Both Psalms are in the form of a question and answer, signifying the conditions for entering the sanctuary of God. This privilege is based on the graciousness of God. Therefore the answers (**Pss 15:2-5b; 24:4-6**) "should not be understood as requirements; rather, they portray the character of persons whose lives have been shaped in conformity with God's character" (**McCann, Book, 733**). McCann points out that the descriptions used here are used elsewhere to describe God (**Ps 18:30**—blameless; **Ps 11:7**—righteous; **Ex 34:6**—faithful) (**ibid.**). God's people reflect His holiness. In both passages it is obvious that these inward traits necessary for the worshiper to enter God's presence are manifested in outward actions.

At times, churches have tried to make entrance into the presence of God easily accessible. There is much talk from those in leadership about the worship leader "bringing us into the presence of God." This task is specifically tied to music in many instances.

The heart of the worshiper is far more important than the choice of the music.

The Psalmist reminds us that "entering His presence is no casual matter" (**ibid., 69**). The heart of the worshiper is far more important than the choice of the music.

A PLACE TO RESPOND

As we have seen, OT worshipers responded to God, the Creator, in multifaceted ways, awed by a God who not only created but intervened. Until the time of the exodus from Egypt, the Israelites worshiped most frequently in family groups.[16] But as congregational worship began to develop, God issued this decree: *"Then have them make a sanctuary for me, and I will dwell among them. Make this tabernacle and all its furnishings exactly like the pattern I will show you"* (***Ex 25:8-9***).

Andrew Hill says, "Through sign, symbol, color, and liturgy the tabernacle served to instruct the Hebrews in God's holiness, transcendence, immanence, wrath and mercy, justice and grace, and covenant love and faithfulness" (**173**). This dwelling place of God provides us with the richness of symbolism and ritual. When the temple later replaced the tabernacle, it continued to remind the Israelites of God's presence among them. These sacred spaces give us insight into God's creativity embodied in earthly form and substance.

The Tabernacle

God gave Moses instructions for the building of the tabernacle, which was to become the center of Israel's worship. Nearly one third of Exodus is concerned with bringing these instructions to fruition, suggesting that, "at least from the narrator's perspective, Israel's experience at Sinai can in no way be regarded as complete without the plans for the tabernacle" (**Balentine, 136**).

A Place for God to Dwell

God wanted a place to dwell among His people (***Ex 25:8***).

---

[16] See Noah, ***Gen 8:10***; Abraham, ***Gen 12:7,8; 13:4,18***.

J. Carl Laney maintains, "This command made possible God's promise to restore Himself to His people. Since Eden, humanity had wandered the world apart from the divine presence. Then at Mount Sinai, God returned His presence and reestablished the long lost relationship of a Creator-King to His subjects. The building of a sanctuary as a place for His holy presence would enshrine His purpose to make His people a kingdom of priests" (9). For the Israelites the tabernacle "constitutes a change in the way God is present among them—ongoing rather than occasional; close, not distant; on-the-move, not fixed" (Birch, 129). Remarking that God's presence in Israel is kingly, William Dumbrell suggests that the presence of the tabernacle is a reminder of Israel's appropriate response to her King, stating that "worship is the protocol by which one may enter the divine presence" (42).

It is important to note that the tabernacle was built in accordance with God's plans. He gave specific details that were to be followed to the letter. Just as God is the one who calls us to worship, He also determines how it should be done.

> **Just as God is the one who calls us to worship, He also determines how it should be done.**

Sacred Space

The building of the tabernacle indicates that there can be space that has spiritual significance. The key to using space appropriately is to acknowledge the way in which it reflects God the Creator and His redemptive purposes. Putting a name on a building does not make a space sacred, nor does the use of particular objects or furniture. Space is sacred when it is given over to God's use, reflects His creativity, communicates with meaningful symbols, and is filled with His presence by virtue of the presence of His people.

The tabernacle housed God's presence; it was not a place that accommodated large gatherings. Worshipers brought their gifts there, which were offered by the priests. The taber-

> **Space is sacred when given over to God's use and filled with His presence through that of His people.**

nacle was symbolically arranged: the Israelites, for the most part, resided in the outer circle, the courtyard was for a higher level of persons, and the Holy Place was limited to a certain number of priests. The Holy of Holies, where the Ark of the Covenant rested, could be accessed only by the High Priest, and only after purification rituals.

The furniture, also built according to God's design, was infused with meaning as well. The Ark of the Covenant symbolized the divine presence. It contained the tablets of the Ten Commandments, a pot of manna, and Aaron's rod. The altar of incense represented prayers; the table of showbread, eaten by priests only, showed that God desired to commune with His people; the lampstand provided light which symbolized God as the only source of light; the bronze laver, where the priests washed before sacrificial offerings was representative of the need for preparation and purification before entering the presence of God.[17]

Transcendence and Immanence

God is "self-existent and self-sufficient" or transcendent. In the OT, this characteristic was often illustrated by direct encounters with Him, known as theophanies. Moses' experience at the burning bush (*Ex 3:2*), his meeting with God at the foot of Mt. Sinai (*Ex 19:16-20*), and the glory that filled the tabernacle (*Ex 40:34-36*) are well-known examples. These face-to-face experiences illustrate that God is "holy other": *"Take off your sandals, for the place you are standing is holy ground." "Go down and warn the people so they do not force their way through to see the LORD and many of them perish." "Moses could not enter the Tent of Meeting because the cloud had settled upon it."* The presence of God Almighty discloses the insignificance of mere men.

---

[17] For a concise description and explanation of the tabernacle furnishings, see **Hill, 166-170.**

Yet God is also characterized by immanence, His "all-pervading presence and power within His creation." Unlike the pagan gods worshiped by the ancients, the God of Israel was, from the very beginning, involved with His creation: *"Who is like the LORD our God, the One who sits enthroned on high, who stoops down to look on the heavens and the earth?"* (**Ps 113:5-6**).

Stanley Grenz and Roger Olson recognize the "challenge of articulating the Christian understanding of the nature of God in a manner that balances, affirms and holds in creative tension the twin truths of the divine transcendence and the divine immanence" (**11**). In his thoughts concerning Exodus, Gerald Janzen discusses the correlation between these two truths. "If," he says, "the laws of *20:22–23:33* are associated with the majesty of God that inspires great fear and a sense of God's distance, the instructions for the sanctuary in *chapters 25–31* are associated with the sense of the communing nearness of God in *24:9-11*" (**185**). Similarly, the tabernacle itself stood as a testimony to the character of a God so great as to be feared, yet within its walls lay the means by which "Israel was enabled to approach the Holy One and to live in His presence" (**Peterson, 32**).

Evangelical gatherings today lean, for the most part, toward immanence, rather than transcendence. Barry Liesch appeals for balance between the two, acknowledging that "given the loss of a sense of transcendence in our culture generally, we will have to work harder to make sure it is present in our worship" (**27**).

A Motif of Offering

At the heart of the plans for the tabernacle is a motif of offering. First, the establishment of a place for God to dwell among His people is "not a human device, but a holy gift that comes from God's own awesome intentionality" (**Brueggemann,**

> **The establishment of a place for God to dwell among His people is no mere human device.**

"Exodus," 882). Second, the building of the tabernacle provided opportunity for the grateful Israelites to give of themselves in honor of Yahweh (*Ex 25:1-2*). "The call for material," says Stephen Binz, "is prefaced by the instruction that all contributions are to be made freely—not compelled—as each one's heart is prompted to give" (98). So willing were they, God had to call a halt to their offerings *"because what they already had was more than enough to do all the work"* (*Ex 36:7*). Finally, the sacrificial system constituted the procedures of worship practiced within the tabernacle, including ritual washings, burnt offerings, prayers of confession or praise, silent meditation or singing of liturgical responses, blessings or benedictions, and a fellowship meal (see **Hill, 142**). Each of these features carries an inference of giving. Implications for Sunday morning worship are evident in this propensity toward offering. Worship is a gift that God gives His children; we need to have a means of responding to Him. Conversely, God desires our worship, which we give willingly, abundantly, and with excellence. In His choice of worship practices God allows for the giftedness and creativity of His people to be used for His glory.

A Feast for the Senses

⁴Moses said to the whole Israelite community, "This is what the LORD has commanded: ⁵From what you have, take an offering for the LORD. Everyone who is willing is to bring to the LORD an offering of gold, silver and bronze; ⁶blue, purple and scarlet yarn and fine linen; goat hair; ⁷ram skins dyed red and hides of sea cows; acacia wood; ⁸olive oil for the light; spices for the anointing oil and for the fragrant incense; ⁹and onyx stones and other gems to be mounted on the ephod and breastpiece." (Ex 35:4-9)

Janzen writes, "The mere listing of the materials for the tabernacle—rich and varied in colors, textures, and aromas—already stimulates the imagination to anticipate the sanctuary as a feast for the senses" (194). He continues, "The tabernacle becomes a place where worship arises to God not just from the human heart and the human spirit but also from the human body as engaged through its various senses and the emotions connected to them" (**ibid.**). Here we encounter the use of the whole self in worship, as we have already seen illustrated in the Psalms.

Artistry is abundantly evident in the design of the tabernacle, and later, the temple. Because artistic expression was part of the ancient world in every culture, the Israelites had no trouble providing the necessary skills to craft the beautiful furnishings and accoutrements required for the completion of these structures.[18] These artistic gifts were inspired by the Spirit of God:

> [30]*Then Moses said to the Israelites, "See, the* LORD *has chosen Bezalel son of Uri, the son of Hur, of the tribe of Judah,* [31]*and he has filled him with the Spirit of God, with skill, ability and knowledge in all kinds of crafts —* [32]*to make artistic designs for work in gold, silver and bronze,* [33]*to cut and set stones, to work in wood and to engage in all kinds of artistic craftsmanship.* (**Ex 35:30-33**)*

Certainly the Israelites understood that their contributions were honoring to the Lord, and did not see these offerings as an end in themselves, but as offerings to God, the Creator.

The transition from the tabernacle to the temple marks a significant era in the worship of Israel, under the leadership of King David. It is this period that gives rise to an organized musical community, designated worship responsibilities for the priesthood, and eventually, a permanent worship structure.

An Organized Worshiping Community

The capture of the Ark of the Covenant by the Philistines (*1Sa 4:1-11*) represented not only a significant defeat in battle, but dealt a blow to the worship of Israel as well. The symbol of the divine presence of God was now in the hands of the enemy. Of course, after seven months of plagues, the

---

[18] See **Hill**, 214, for a list of arts, skills, and crafts used by the Israelites.

Philistines were ready to return it. It was sent to Beth Shemesh, where seventy men were struck dead for looking at it. The ark then found a resting place for twenty years at Kiriath Jearim until David transferred it to Jerusalem, but not without the expense of the life of Uzzah, who touched it when it was in danger of falling (*2Sa 6:1-11* and *1Chr 13:1-13*).

It is not surprising that bringing the ark to Jerusalem was an occasion for worship, including singing, dancing, and sacrifice.[19] David placed the ark in a specifically prepared tent located in Zion, where the worship surrounding its installation included burnt offerings and fellowship offerings (*1Sa 6:17-18*). After these initial rituals, however, worship at David's tent was characterized by praise, including singing, prophesying, and playing musical instruments (*1Chr 16:4; 25:1-31*). It is likely that many of the Psalms were both written and used in the worship surrounding David's tent (**J. Leonard, "Tabernacle,"** 121). The return of the ark to the midst of God's people allowed for the establishment of a center of worship for Israel.

David desired to build a permanent structure to house the ark, but was denied the privilege (*2Sa 7:1-17; 1Chr 28:1-7*). God did, however, entrust David with planning the house that Solomon would build. Again, as in the building of the tabernacle, God gave specific instructions for its construction. *"All this,"* David said, *"I have in writing from the hand of the LORD upon me, and he gave me understanding in all the details of the plan"* (*1Chr 28:19*). The organization of worship in the time of David leaves no doubt that God desired to have a say in how He would be worshiped. *"All this"* (*1Chr 28:19*) included not just the plans for the temple itself, but the plans for worshiping there.

Near the end of his life, after turning the kingship over to Solomon, David gathered the Levites and set them aside to

---

[19] The response of David's wife, Michal, is notable. She *"despised him in her heart"* (*2Sa 6:16*). She was punished for this attitude by not being blessed with children.

perform the important ministry of worship leadership. The descendants of the tribe of Levi had been in charge of the tabernacle, setting it up and tearing it down, as well as caring for its furniture, including the Ark of the Covenant (*Num 1:47-54*). They also assisted the priests in acts of worship, such as consecrating the bread, looking after tithes and offerings, and preparing sacrifices. In short, they were trusted with the holy things of worship, which was no small matter. Now that the building of a permanent worship structure was imminent, David divided 38,000 Levites who were over thirty years of age into groups of 24,000 for the work of the temple, 6,000 as officials and judges, 4,000 as gatekeepers, and 4,000 as musicians (*1Chr 23:1-5*).[20]

We have already seen that music played an important part in the worship of the Israelites. It is at this juncture, however, that it becomes organized and mandated. According to 1 Chronicles:

> [1]*David, together with the commanders of the army, set apart some of the sons of Asaph, Heman and Jeduthun for the ministry of prophesying, accompanied by harps, lyres and cymbals. . . . [6]All these men were under the supervision of their fathers for the music of the temple of the LORD, with cymbals, lyres and harps, for the ministry at the house of God. Asaph, Jeduthun and Heman were under the supervision of the king. [7]Along with their relatives—all of them trained and skilled in music for the LORD—they numbered 288. (*1Chr 25:1,6-7*)*

Music played an important part in the worship of the Israelites.

Hill suggests, "These musical guilds were responsible for composing and directing the songs of praise and thanksgiving used in the temple celebrations and worship services" (**40**). The musicians stayed in the Temple and were responsible for the work *"day and night"* (*1Chr 9:33*). The picture of leadership that we see here is the closest biblical example we

---

[20] Music also is prominent at the rebuilding of the temple in Ezra and Nehemiah.

have to our 21st-century definition of worship ministry. In that regard, several observations are of value.

First, the musicians were selected from among the Levites. Their *spiritual* qualifications were more important than their *musical* qualifications. Levites had to be purified and consecrated before performing their various ministries (see **Num 8:6-21**). They had been set apart, and were expected to reflect the holiness of God.

Second, their ministry included prophesying, not just singing and playing instruments, which implies that some sort of divine revelation was inherent in their calling.[21] Richard Leonard suggests that "these musicians led in a spontaneous and overwhelming outpouring of worship" (**"Prophetic,"** 165-166). This responsibility gave the musicians a status above the ordinary Levites, but below the priests, indicating the importance that God placed upon the use of music in worship. Their ministry was one of both praise and exhortation.

Third, both vocal and instrumental music were considered to be valuable for worship. We have noted the obvious presence of instruments in the Psalms, but the worship of the temple solidifies them as useful and appropriate. Harps, lyres, tambourines, cymbals, and trumpets were employed for praise when the ark was moved to Jerusalem (*1Chr 13:8*). Apparently instrumental music was not always accompanied by verbal praise: *"Heman and Jeduthun were responsible for the sounding of the trumpets and cymbals and for the playing of the other instruments for sacred song"* (*1Chr 16:42*). Other times, however, the two joined together in a spirit of unity:

---

[21] See *1Sa 10:15*: *"After that you will go to Gibeah of God, where there is a Philistine outpost. As you approach the town, you will meet a procession of prophets coming down from the high place with lyres, tambourines, flutes and harps being played before them, and they will be prophesying."* Asaph is called a "seer," one who received divine messages in visions or dreams (*2Chr 29:30*), as was Heman (*1Chr 25:5*). Miriam and Deborah, both prophetesses, composed songs as a means of praising God for victory (*Exodus 15; Jdg 4:4*). Peter quotes David in his Pentecost sermon, calling the singer of Israel a prophet (*Acts 2:25-31*). Prophesying could include speaking for God, involving not only new revelations, but also reminders of old revelations.

> ¹²*All the Levites who were musicians—Asaph, Heman, Jeduthun and their sons and relatives—stood on the east side of the altar, dressed in fine linen and playing cymbals, harps and lyres. They were accompanied by 120 priests sounding trumpets. ¹³The trumpeters and singers joined in unison, as with one voice, to give praise and thanks to the LORD. Accompanied by trumpets, cymbals and other instruments, they raised their voices in praise to the LORD and sang:*
>
>> *"He is good;*
>> *his love endures forever." (2Chr 5:12-13).*

Finally, the elaborate worship gatherings required that the musicians of David's day be trained, skilled, and supervised. Their duties required that they work unselfishly together. *First Chronicles 25:8* states, *"Young and old alike, teacher as well as student, cast lots for their duties."* All of the musicians were qualified, but casting lots ensured that the order in which they served was determined by God. There was no favoritism, but rather an expectation of excellence and partnership for the music used in the service of the Lord. Later, the musicians were placed in charge of the workers who repaired the temple under the leadership of Josiah (*2Chr 34:12-13*).

The Temple

When Solomon completed the temple and was able to place the ark there, along with the tabernacle furniture, the occasion was momentous:

> ¹⁰*When the priests withdrew from the Holy Place, the cloud filled the temple of the LORD. ¹¹And the priests could not perform their service because of the cloud, for the glory of the LORD filled His temple. ¹²Then Solomon said, "The LORD has said that he would dwell in a dark cloud; ¹³I have indeed built a magnificent temple for you, a place for you to dwell forever. (1Kgs 8:10-13)*

During the reign of Solomon, the temple "took over the visual function of the tabernacle. It was a place where people under the old covenant had the opportunity to develop their relationship with God through sacrifice and prayer. Everything in it served to remind God's people that sin separates them from a holy God" (**Laney, 37**). The temple was larger and more extravagant than the tabernacle, but still reminded the people of God's presence among them.[22] While the tabernacle was portable, the temple was permanent, indicating "the transition from a wandering people to an established kingdom" (**Longman, *Immanuel*, 47-48**).

Since kings frequently built temples in honor of their gods, it must have seemed appropriate to the people of Israel to also erect such a structure. Yahweh, however, was in no need of one (see *1Kgs 8:27; Acts 7:48-50*). His divine wisdom though, acknowledged that His people needed a tangible reminder of His faithfulness. Furthermore, a place to offer sacrifices was necessary for covenant keeping, obedience, and loyalty.

Prayer and Sacrifice

Solomon's prayer of dedication brings to light an emphasis not prevalent in the worship of the tabernacle, that of a place of prayer:

> **A place to offer sacrifices was necessary for covenant keeping, obedience, and loyalty.**

> [28]*Yet give attention to your servant's prayer and his plea for mercy, O LORD my God. Hear the cry and the prayer that your servant is praying in your presence this day. [29]May your eyes be open toward this temple night and day, this place of which you said, "My Name shall be there," so that you will hear the prayer your servant prays toward this place. [30]Hear the supplication of your servant and of your people Israel when they pray toward this place. Hear from heaven, your dwelling place, and when you hear, forgive.*
> (*1Kgs 8:28-30*)

Solomon recognizes that even though God's people may pray toward the temple, He will answer from heaven, where He dwells. This prayer of dedication and the acts that surround also emphasize the importance of sacred space.

---

[22] See *1 Kings 5–8* for a portrait of the temple.

Under Solomon's reign the temple also became the place for the ritual of sacrifices (*2Chr 7:11-12*), "visible and tangible expressions of the relationship of God's people with himself" (**Webber, *Features*, 129**). The sacrificial system will be discussed in an upcoming chapter.

Symbolism

Robert Webber emphasizes that the arrangement of the outer court, inner court, and Holy of Holies, as well as the various pieces of furniture "were laden with symbolic meaning as they depicted an encounter with God" (**Webber, *Features*, 129**).[23] This attention to the symbolic had been true of the tabernacle as well. Both model "the use of sign and symbol in artistic expression to convey theological truths" (**Hill, 190**).[24]

> **In the ancient world a symbol had the ability to embody what it symbolized.**

For most people today, symbols are mere representations or illustrations of something else. But in the ancient world they were "not merely notions; they were powerful mediators of divine activity"(**Webber, *History*, 79**). In other words, a symbol had the ability to embody the thing that it symbolized; thus, in biblical history the divine presence was made visible through signs and symbols. Ron Owens illustrates:

> As we follow the pilgrimage of the children of Israel in the OT, we see God expressing various aspects of His nature and giving different pictures of what He is like. He revealed, or imaged, Himself at the foot of Mount Sinai with the cloud and the fire. He imaged His character in the Ten Commandments. He imaged Himself in the Ark of the Covenant, in which were placed the rod and bread. The seat on top of the ark represented the throne. The ark itself imaged the intimate bond that He had established between Himself and His people, and it

[23] The tabernacle furniture was moved by Solomon into the temple (*1Kgs 8:4*).
[24] For the difference between sign and symbol in the OT see **Hill, 57-58**.

was placed in the Holy of Holies where His *shekinah* glory, His presence, dwelt. . . . The entire Old Testament preimaged the Son. Everything pointed toward Him until, in the fullness of time, He, in whom all the fullness of the Godhead dwelt, would be fleshed out among us. God's primary and complete image of Himself was revealed in Jesus Christ. (**23**)

Other symbols found in the Bible include the rainbow, altars, sanctuaries, the burning bush, cloud by day, fire by night, circumcision, unleavened bread, the Cross, tongues of fire, the Eucharist, baptism, and the Church. William Robinson calls attention to the fact that for the Jew "the Word of God was never primarily a spoken word. It was given in *act* rather than in phrase" (**217**). He continues, "In worship, which was corporate action, rather than words, Christians constantly saw the holy action of God re-presented in symbolic forms" (**219**).

Barry Liesch states that the "symbolic meanings provide us with insights into many aspects of our own worship" (**140**). Noting that many churches have tended to value verbal over symbolic, he contends that "it may not be enough to provide people with an intellectual faith and an intellectual worship that centers on verbal expression. . . . The spatial and symbolical may be as crucial as the verbal and analytic" (**145**).

THE LAMENTS

Sometimes we may feel confused or even abandoned by our Creator because His ways are not our ways. The Scriptural response to this is lament, which Hill describes as an "expression of honest doubt about God's goodness and an appeal to God's grace and compassion for intervention in a desperate situation" (**198**). These have been all but abandoned in our current culture. Many planners of Sunday gatherings have faced this dilemma following a tragedy within their particular community. In America, our lack of repertoire became obvious on the Sunday following the attacks of

September 11, 2001. There were no hymns or praise choruses that adequately expressed the grief and confusion felt by most people seated in pews that day.

Scripture, however, does not shy away from the human need to cry, question, and despair. The Psalms in particular provide numerous accounts of such expressions.[25] John Witvliet implores, "When faced with an utter loss of words and an oversupply of volatile emotions, we best rely not on our own stuttering speech but on the reliable and profoundly relevant laments of the Hebrew Scriptures" (42).

> **Scripture does not shy away from the human need to cry, question, and despair.**

Take, for example, the desperate cry of David in Psalm 56:

> [1]Be merciful to me, O God, for men hotly pursue me;
>   all day long they press their attack.
> [2]My slanderers pursue me all day long;
>   many are attacking me in their pride.
> [3]When I am afraid,
>   I will trust in you.
> [4]In God, whose word I praise,
>   in God I trust; I will not be afraid.
>   What can mortal man do to me?
> [5]All day long they twist my words;
>   they are always plotting to harm me.
> [6]They conspire, they lurk,
>   they watch my steps,
>   eager to take my life.
> [7]On no account let them escape;
>   in your anger, O God, bring down the nations.
> [8]Record my lament;
>   list my tears on your scroll—
>   are they not in your record?
> [9]Then my enemies will turn back
>   when I call for help.
>   By this I will know that God is for me.

---

[25] According to Tremper Longman III, lament is "the predominant genre of the Psalter, with as many as fifty examples of individual laments and twenty examples of corporate laments" ("Lament," 203).

[10]In God, whose word I praise,
  in the LORD, whose word I praise—
[11] in God I trust; I will not be afraid.
  What can man do to me?
[12]I am under vows to you, O God;
  I will present my thank offerings to you.
For you have delivered me from death
  and my feet from stumbling,
that I may walk before God
  in the light of life. (Ps 56:1-13)

The Psalms of lament have a distinctive structure that includes an opening address (such as "O God"), a description of the complaint, a plea for God's response, a profession of trust, and a promise to praise or offer a sacrifice to God (**McCann, *Book*, 644-645**). Reflecting on *Psalm 56*, McCann notes that it and other such prayers teach us "that human life is always lived under threat, in the midst of opposition, either from ourselves or from others or from some external circumstance. The good news, however, is that because God

Because God is for us we can say, "I am not afraid."

is for us (see *v. 9*), we can say with the psalmist, 'I am not afraid'" (**McCann, *Book*, 903**).

Long ignored in most Christian Churches, the laments offer an alternative to the modern-day insistence upon expressions of worship that highlight only praise. Many enter churches each Sunday afraid, confused, and perhaps in doubt about the ability of God to intervene. Some claim that there is no absolute truth, yet still come seeking answers. The laments give outlet to the fears of the lost and show them that they are not alone.

NEW TESTAMENT RESPONSE

NEW TESTAMENT VOCABULARY

The study of worship responses in the NT requires an examination of vocabulary, in particular two Greek words, *proskuneo* and *latreuo*. These correspond to the Hebrew words that denote bowing down and service, respectively.[26] *Proskuneo* is found over fifty times in the NT, most prominently in the Gospels and Revelation.[27] An appropriate understanding of the word includes action, such as bowing, prostrating, or kissing toward, as well as homage and reverence. Heinrich Greeven points out that in the NT use of *proskuneo* "the object is always something—truly or supposedly—divine." (763). In the NT it is the presence of the Almighty that invokes worship: "The Son of God was visible to all on earth (the Gospels) and the exalted Lord will again be visible to His own when faith gives way to sight (Revelation)" (765). While the physical aspect is prominent in the NT, *proskuneo* can also "denote the corresponding inward attitude of reverence and humility" (Schönweiss, 876).

It is in the Book of Revelation that we see the most vivid portrayal of worship, often in a form of hymnic expression, confirming that ultimate praise is reserved for the triune God alone, and that it occurs unceasingly in His presence.

> **It is in the Book of Revelation that we see the most vivid portrayal of worship.**

> [5]*From the throne came flashes of lightning, rumblings and peals of thunder. Before the throne, seven lamps were blazing. These are the seven spirits of God. (**Rev 4:5**)*[28]

> [8]*Each of the four living creatures had six wings and was covered with eyes all around, even under his wings. Day and night they never stop saying:*
> *"Holy, holy, holy*

---

[26] *Shachah* and *'abad*.

[27] As we shall see in chapter 4, *proskuneo* is used most prolifically by Jesus in **John 4**. Other examples include **Mt 2:2,8,11; Rev 4:8-11; 5:8-10,12-14; 7:10-12; 11:15-18; 12:10ff; 15:3; 16:5-7; 19:1-7.** In **Mt 4:9; Rev 13:4,8,12,15; 16:2; 19:10; 22:8,9** the usage does not refer to the worship of God. Paul uses *proskuneo* only once, in **1Cor 14:25**. The writer of Hebrews quotes the OT, **Heb 1:6; 11:21**.

[28] See **Rev 1:4**; "the seven spirits of God" represent the Holy Spirit. "With God the Father seated on the throne and the Holy Spirit represented by the seven lamps, the stage was then set for the revelation (**chap. 5**) of Christ Himself as the slain Lamb" (Walvoord, 943).

*is the Lord God Almighty,
who was, and is, and is to come." (**Rev 4: 8**)*

*The twenty-four elders and the four living creatures fell
down and worshiped God, who was seated on the throne.
And they cried: "Amen, Hallelujah!" (**Rev 19:4**)*

In the NT acceptable worship involves application to one's
lifestyle as is evidenced by the Greek word, *latreuo*. The basic
meaning is "to work or serve for reward." A few of its occur-
rences are translated "worship,"[29] while the remainder are rendered "serve." It sometimes refers to serving the Lord through
the devout and upright life (**Rom 1:9; 12:1**), but can also refer
more specifically to worshiping in a corporate sense. Lynn
Hieronymus says that the "essence of this word [*latreuo*] is in
its reference to the acts or duties that one performs in the overall role of worship, for example, the act in the ancient day of
offering sacrifice or burning incense" (**44-45**).

NEW TESTAMENT ATTITUDES

For those who had gained new life in Christ, the attitude
of constant thanksgiving became a hallmark of worship. In
Romans 1:21, Paul has harsh words for those who did not
honor God in this way: *"For
although they knew God, they neither glorified him as God nor gave
thanks to him, but their thinking
became futile and their foolish
hearts were darkened."*

> **For those who had new
> life in Christ, constant
> thanksgiving became a
> hallmark of worship.**

In other Epistles, Paul repeatedly commends thanksgiving to his readers:

*Give thanks in all circumstances, for this is God's will for
you in Christ Jesus. (**1Th 5:18**)*

*And whatever you do, whether in word or deed, do it all in
the name of the Lord Jesus, giving thanks to God the Father
through him. (**Col 3:17**)*

[29] ***Acts 7:42; 24:14; Heb 12:28; Php 3:3; Rom 12:1**, in noun form.*

Hebrews 12:28 offers an example of "acceptable" worship, which also includes an attitude of thankfulness: *"Therefore, since we are receiving a kingdom that cannot be shaken, let us be thankful, and so worship God acceptably with reverence and awe."* In this passage, "be thankful" is more literally translated "have grace" (*charis*). Paul uses the same terminology in **Colossians 3:16**, *"as you sing psalms, hymns and spiritual songs with gratitude [charis] in your hearts to God."* Used in these contexts the word probably refers to being thankful for the benefits that God has provided.

Hand in hand with thanksgiving goes continual rejoicing: *"Rejoice in the Lord always. I will say it again: Rejoice!"* (**Php 4:4**). *"Be joyful always"* (**1Th 5:16**).

Praise is also an earmark of a Christ follower, just as it was to the Israelites of old. A favorite word of Paul is *epainos*,[30] which indicates commendation or approval, specifically given by God or His authorities. More closely associated with worship is *aineo*, which refers to the joyful praise of God in song or prayer.[31] Note that this praise is given by individuals, groups, and angels, and that it is used only of God (and Jesus, in **Lk 19:37**).

Perhaps the best known word for praise in the NT is *doxa*, from which our word "doxology" is derived, most commonly translated as "glory."[32] The OT counterpart of *doxa*, is *kabod*, meaning "weight" or "importance." When applied to God in the OT, there was frequently some kind of physical manifestation of God's "weight" or "importance."[33] In the NT, *doxa* is often used to describe "the revelation of the character and the presence of God in the Person and work of Jesus Christ" (**Nixon, 415**). Luke, for example, records the shepherds' reaction to the physical presence of the glory of God:

---

[30] *Rom 2:29; 13:3; 1Cor 4:5; 2Cor 8:18; Eph 1:6,12,14; Php 1:11; 4:8.*
[31] *Lk 2:13,20; 19:37; 24:53; Acts 2:47; 3:8,9; Rom 15:11; Rev 19:5.*
[32] *Lk 2:9,14; Jn 1:14; Rom 11:36; 2Cor 3:18; Eph 1:6,12,14,17,18; Php 4:19,20; Col 1:27; Rev 4:9,11; 5:12,13.* In both verb and noun form this word is used over 200 times in the NT.
[33] *Ex 16:10; 40:34; Num 16:19; Ezek 10:4.*

> *[8]And there were shepherds living out in the fields nearby, keeping watch over their flocks at night. [9]An angel of the Lord appeared to them, and the glory of the Lord shone around them, and they were terrified. (Lk 2:8-9)*

Not only is glory a characteristic of God, but we as humans are required to give Him glory, a response exemplified by the angels in the above encounter:

We as humans are required to give God glory.

> *[13]Suddenly a great company of the heavenly host appeared with the angel, praising God and saying, [14]"Glory to God in the highest, and on earth peace to men on whom His favor rests." (Lk 2:13-14)*

According to Paul, failure to glorify God causes Him to turn sinful men over to their desires:

> *[21]For since the creation of the world God's invisible qualities—His eternal power and divine nature—have been clearly seen, being understood from what has been made, so that men are without excuse. For although they knew God, they neither glorified him as God nor gave thanks to him, but their thinking became futile and their foolish hearts were darkened. [22]Although they claimed to be wise, they became fools [23]and exchanged the glory of the immortal God for images made to look like mortal man and birds and animals and reptiles. [24]Therefore God gave them over in the sinful desires of their hearts to sexual impurity for the degrading of their bodies with one another. [25]They exchanged the truth of God for a lie, and worshiped and served created things rather than the Creator—who is forever praised. Amen. (Rom 1:21-25)*

CONCLUSION

Recognizing God as Creator puts into context our role in the worship story. Fergusson states, "We ourselves are part of a larger history. Our human story is situated within the narrative of creation. Our identity and destiny cannot be understood apart from that of the cosmos" (**6**).

But often, it seems, we begin our corporate gatherings with ourselves instead of the Creator. What do we want, need, or like? Sometimes, perhaps, we put ourselves in the role of creator. If we sing or say this or that, create a certain atmosphere, make ourselves comfortable, then surely God will make Himself known. The God who created the heavens and the earth most certainly deserves more than that.

Stephen Charnock, a Puritan minister who lived in the seventeenth century, observed the danger of setting ourselves above God.

> To pretend a homage to God, and intend only the advantage of self, is rather to mock Him than to worship Him. When we believe that we ought to be satisfied rather than God be glorified, we set God below ourselves, imagine that He should submit His own honor to our advantage. So we make ourselves more glorious than God, as though we were not made for Him, but He hath a being only for us; this is to have a very low esteem of the majesty of God. (148-149)

Worship is a human response to a Divine initiative.

God, the Creator, is seen throughout Scripture as the object of worship. This worship is a human response to a Divine initiative. Whether in the cultic worship of ancient Israel, the face-to-face encounters with God in the Gospels, the lifestyle responses of the early Church, or the cosmic praise around the Throne, our 21st-century worship finds words and actions worthy of emulating.

"What Do You Say" about the topics discussed in this chapter?
To aid your discussion, see the box on the next page.

What Do You Say?

1. Which aspects of OT worship are prevalent in our present day gatherings? Which are absent? Which should be recovered?

2. Are we guilty of making ourselves "more glorious than God"? If so, give examples of how this attitude might be manifested in our gatherings.

3. How might the tabernacle and the temple influence our thinking about sacred space today?

4. Can you think of an instance when lamenting would have been appropriate in your context? How might this have been accomplished? What would it have done for the body of believers?

5. In what ways could we use our creativity to honor the Creator in corporate worship? In personal worship?

The Drama of Redemption

I refer to Easter, 1993, as the day they crucified Lee Hinkle. Now I presume that none of you know Lee, but if you did, you would probably be thinking, "I'm sure he did something to deserve it." But no, what he did was portray Jesus in the Easter Pageant at Highland Meadows Christian Church in Colleyville, Texas.

Up to that point in my life I had seen the crucifixion acted out in dozens of pageants or movies by as many different actors. But on that night, as I watched the horrible events being recalled, I recognized the face. Lee was a student at Dallas Christian College where I taught at the time. We had been on choir tours together where all you have to do is sit on the bus and talk. One summer night Lee (the intern) and I (the part-time music minister) ran Sunday evening church while all the other ministers were on vacation, then I gave him a ride—to the North American Christian Convention in Denver, Colorado. During choir tour one year we spent a day at Disney World together. Lee Hinkle was my friend.

*I knew that the blood wasn't real, there weren't real thorns in that crown being pushed into his flesh, the whipping and scourging were fake, and the nails were not really being driven into his hands and feet. But still, it was difficult to watch, and I knew that if it **were** real, I would not be sitting calmly in my cold metal chair but would be right there begging them to stop. I knew this man—he was my friend!*

I put myself in the place of the disciples that long ago day, helpless at the foot of the cross—"we know this man—He is our friend!"

I wonder then, how we sit calmly in our padded pews Sunday after Sunday and speak, sing, and remember the redemptive story with so little recognition of the sacrifice it required. When we participate in the Lord's Supper, do we see the representation of the body and the blood of my friend, and yours? These actions are not banal reminders of long ago events. They bring to life the victorious work of our Lord Jesus Christ, the amazing truth that we are no longer helpless at the foot of the cross; we are empowered there!

The Lord Jesus Himself wanted us never to forget, never to take for granted, never to ignore, never to underestimate the sacrifice, the love, and the triumph.

"I know this man—He is my friend!" Greater love has no one than this, that he lay down his life for his friends.

CHAPTER TWO

GOD, THE REDEEMER

*But now, this is what the L*ORD *says—*
He who created you, O Jacob,
He who formed you, O Israel,
"Fear not, for I have redeemed you;
I have summoned you by name; you are mine."
Isaiah 43:1

Retelling the Bible's story line brings to mind again and again something of God's character, past actions, and words. It calls to mind God's great redemptive acts across the panorama of redemptive history. This perspective is frequently lost in contemporary worship, where there are very few elements calculated to make us remember the great turning points in the Bible. (**Carson, 33**)

THE RELATIONSHIP OF REDEMPTION TO ISRAEL'S WORSHIP

Then say to him, 'The LORD, the God of the Hebrews, has sent me to say to you: *Let my people go, so that they may worship me.'"*[1] Six times God extends

[1] **Ex 7:16; 8:1,20; 9:1,13; 10:3.** In these passages the Hebrew *'abad*, "serve," is rendered in the LXX by *latreuo*. According to Klaus Hess, when Moses asks Pharaoh to let the people go so that they may "serve" God in the desert, "it is a question of worship, which, as in the case of other ancient peoples, was carried out through the cultus" (550). *Continued on next page*

this admonition to Pharaoh as he appeals to the ruler for the release of the Israelites. God desired His children to be free to worship Him only; thus, Israel's release from bondage became the crux of their worship. The importance of the exodus event to developing a strong biblical basis for corporate worship cannot be overstated.

William Dumbrell emphasizes that the book of Exodus moves from "Israel enslaved to Israel at worship" (**39**). He continues, "Israel has been redeemed *from* Pharaoh, but redeemed *for* Yahweh" (**39**). Just as one God who is Creator of all things stands apart from other gods, so does a God who intervenes and redeems.

Isaiah repeatedly recalls the significance of God as Redeemer:

> [6]"This is what the LORD says—
>> Israel's King and Redeemer, the LORD Almighty:
> I am the first and I am the last;
>> apart from me there is no God.
> [7]Who then is like me? Let him proclaim it.
>> Let him declare and lay out before me
> what has happened since I established my ancient people,
>> and what is yet to come—
>> yes, let him foretell what will come.
> [8]Do not tremble, do not be afraid.
>> Did I not proclaim this and foretell it long ago?
> You are my witnesses. Is there any God besides me?
>> No, there is no other Rock; I know not one."
>
> (**Isa 44:6-8**)[2]

Redemption means to deliver from calamity of some kind by paying a price. For the Israelites, the redemption

Some writers use the words *cult* or *cultic* in reference to OT worship to denote the worship practices of a specific group. From the Latin, *cultus*, the original meaning is "worship" or "formal religious veneration." This usage should not be confused with the contemporary use of the word to refer to heretical religious groups.

[2] See also **Isa 41:14; 43:14; 44:24; 47:4; 48:17; 49:7,26; 54:5,8; 59:20; 60:16; 63:16**.

from the clutches of Pharaoh in Egypt became the essence of the story that continues to be retold again and again.

The children of Israel, far removed chronologically from the exodus event, could still recall the saving deeds of Yahweh as part of their public gatherings, thus expressing their verbal acts of worship both individually and corporately. It was not merely a onetime event that was celebrated. Rather, "Israel's worship sustained the faith that because God had acted once, He would continue to act for her salvation" (**Williams, 85**).

James Muilenburg condenses Israel's corporate gatherings as follows: "These times which God gives His people are for remembering, for rehearsing in living words, for activating in cultic drama, and for joyous celebration. It is *good* for Israel to be granted this way of life" (**109**). Our worship can be enriched by active attention to the story of redemption.

> **Our worship can be enriched by active attention to the story of redemption.**

RECITAL: LIVING WORDS

We have seen in the previous chapter that a vital and natural response to the nature of Yahweh is praise. The Psalmist(s) reminds us that testifying to God's redeeming work is equally important.

> *One generation will commend your works to another;*
>   *they will tell of your mighty acts.* (**Ps 145:4**)

> *My mouth will tell of your righteousness,*
>   *of your salvation all day long,*
>   *though I know not its measure.* (**Ps 71:15**)

> *I do not hide your righteousness in my heart;*
>   *I speak of your faithfulness and salvation.*
> *I do not conceal your love and your truth*
>   *from the great assembly.* (**Ps 40:10**)

Remembering the Redemption Story

Much of Israel's corporate worship included the recitation of God's saving acts. For example, the following hymn[3] describes Yahweh's intervention when the Israelites found themselves saved from the pursuit of Pharaoh's army:

[1]Then Moses and the Israelites sang this song to the LORD:

"I will sing to the LORD,
for he is highly exalted.
The horse and its rider
he has hurled into the sea.
[2]The LORD is my strength and my song;
he has become my salvation.
He is my God, and I will praise him,
my father's God, and I will exalt him.
[3]The LORD is a warrior
the LORD is his name.
[4]Pharaoh's chariots and his army
he has hurled into the sea.
The best of Pharaoh's officers
are drowned in the Red Sea.
[5]The deep waters have covered them;
they sank to the depths like a stone.
[6]"Your right hand, O LORD,
was majestic in power.
Your right hand, O LORD,
shattered the enemy.
[7]In the greatness of your majesty
you threw down those who opposed you.
You unleashed your burning anger;
it consumed them like stubble.
[8]By the blast of your nostrils
the waters piled up.
The surging waters stood firm like a wall;
the deep waters congealed in the heart of the sea.
[9]"The enemy boasted,
'I will pursue, I will overtake them.
I will divide the spoils;
I will gorge myself on them.

[3]A hymn, in its simplest sense, is a song written in praise of a god or hero.

I will draw my sword
*   and my hand will destroy them.'*
[10]But you blew with your breath,
*   and the sea covered them.*
They sank like lead
*   in the mighty waters.*
[11]"Who among the gods is like you, O LORD?
*   Who is like you—*
*   majestic in holiness,*
*   awesome in glory,*
*   working wonders?*
[12]You stretched out your right hand
*   and the earth swallowed them.*
[13]"In your unfailing love you will lead
*   the people you have redeemed.*
In your strength you will guide them
*   to your holy dwelling.*
[14]The nations will hear and tremble;
*   anguish will grip the people of Philistia.*
[15]The chiefs of Edom will be terrified,
*   the leaders of Moab will be seized with trem-*
*   bling,*
the people of Canaan will melt away;
*   [16]terror and dread will fall upon them.*
By the power of your arm
*   they will be as still as a stone—*
until your people pass by, O LORD,
*   until the people you bought pass by.*
[17]You will bring them in and plant them
*   on the mountain of your inheritance—*
the place, O LORD, you made for your dwelling,
*   the sanctuary, O Lord, your hands established.*
[18]The LORD will reign
*   for ever and ever"* (**Ex 15:1-18**).

Not only is the miraculous feat of God outlined in this canticle, but because of His continued faithfulness to His children, the recitation of His saving acts transcends any given moment in time. The song of *Exodus 15*, claims Göran Larsson, "has never lost its freshness and relevance. For it not only deals

> **The recitation of His saving acts transcends any given moment in time.**

with God's acts of salvation in the past but also proclaims God's power and grace for the future" (106).

The Israelites understood themselves to be part of a bigger picture; their individual responses conveyed a corporate identity. In *Psalm 77*, the Psalmist recalls the miracle of the Red Sea as he seeks God's intervention for his own distress:

¹I cried out to God for help;
    I cried out to God to hear me.
²When I was in distress, I sought the Lord;
    at night I stretched out untiring hands
    and my soul refused to be comforted.
³I remembered you, O God, and I groaned;
    I mused, and my spirit grew faint.
⁴You kept my eyes from closing;
    I was too troubled to speak.
⁵I thought about the former days,
    the years of long ago;
⁶I remembered my songs in the night.
    My heart mused and my spirit inquired:
⁷"Will the Lord reject forever?
    Will he never show his favor again?
⁸Has his unfailing love vanished forever?
    Has his promise failed for all time?
⁹Has God forgotten to be merciful?
    Has he in anger withheld his compassion?"
¹⁰Then I thought, "To this I will appeal:
    the years of the right hand of the Most High."
¹¹I will remember the deeds of the LORD;
    yes, I will remember your miracles of long ago.
¹²I will meditate on all your works
    and consider all your mighty deeds.
¹³Your ways, O God, are holy.
    What god is so great as our God?
¹⁴You are the God who performs miracles;
    you display your power among the peoples.
¹⁵With your mighty arm you redeemed your people,
    the descendants of Jacob and Joseph.
¹⁶The waters saw you, O God,
    the waters saw you and writhed;
    the very depths were convulsed.
¹⁷The clouds poured down water,
    the skies resounded with thunder;
    your arrows flashed back and forth.

*18Your thunder was heard in the whirlwind,
    your lightning lit up the world;
    the earth trembled and quaked.
19Your path led through the sea,
    your way through the mighty waters,
    though your footprints were not seen.
20You led your people like a flock
    by the hand of Moses and Aaron. (**Ps 77:1-20**).*

It is important to understand the corporate nature of Israel's worship.[4] Often the use of the word "I" does not refer only to the person speaking, either in Scripture or in contemporary liturgies. "Due to the intense group-consciousness of the Jewish people, the Jewish prayers are mostly in the first person plural. . . . A great sage of the third century advised the people to include the entire group in one's own prayers. Even the first person singular often used in the Psalms is now commonly interpreted as of collective nature" (**Idelsohn, vi**). The above Psalm, for example, carries the heading, "For the Director of Music," suggesting that it may have been intended for singing in public gatherings. If so, then Asaph, the composer, is speaking for all of Israel. Even Psalms intended to reflect an individual's personal journey "became part of Israel's continuing experience in worship because they reflected a common religious pilgrimage and a shared religious heritage with which those who came to worship across the years could readily identify" (**Davidson, 5**). It is a shared story that makes memory a powerful part of worship.

> **It is a shared story that makes memory a powerful part of worship.**

---

[4] For opposing views on this matter see *Psalms* by Hermann Gunkel, who looked at the Psalms as being more connected to personal spirituality, and *The Psalms in Israel's Worship* by Sigmund Mowinckel, who believed they should be understood according to their use in the corporate worship of Israel.

Remembering through Word and Deed

At times God commanded His children to remember through both word and deed. The following passage is at the heart of Jewish worship:

> [1]These are the commands, decrees and laws the LORD your God directed me to teach you to observe in the land that you are crossing the Jordan to possess, [2]so that you, your children and their children after them may fear the LORD your God as long as you live by keeping all his decrees and commands that I give you, and so that you may enjoy long life. [3]Hear, O Israel, and be careful to obey so that it may go well with you and that you may increase greatly in a land flowing with milk and honey, just as the LORD, the God of your fathers, promised you.
>
> [4]Hear, O Israel: The LORD our God, the LORD is one. [5]Love the LORD your God with all your heart and with all your soul and with all your strength. [6]These commandments that I give you today are to be upon your hearts. [7]Impress them on your children. Talk about them when you sit at home and when you walk along the road, when you lie down and when you get up. [8]Tie them as symbols on your hands and bind them on your foreheads. [9]Write them on the doorframes of your houses and on your gates.
>
> [10]When the LORD your God brings you into the land He swore to your fathers, to Abraham, Isaac and Jacob, to give you—a land with large, flourishing cities you did not build, [11]houses filled with all kinds of good things you did not provide, wells you did not dig, and vineyards and olive groves you did not plant—then when you eat and are satisfied, [12]be careful that you do not forget the LORD, who brought you out of Egypt, out of the land of slavery. . . .
>
> [20]In the future, when your son asks you, "What is the meaning of the stipulations, decrees and laws the LORD our God has commanded you?" [21]tell him: "We were slaves of Pharaoh in Egypt, but the LORD brought us out of Egypt with a mighty hand. [22]Before our eyes the LORD sent miraculous signs and wonders—great and terrible—upon Egypt and Pharaoh and his whole household. [23]But he brought us out from there to bring us in and give us the land that he promised on oath to our forefathers.

> [24]The LORD commanded us to obey all these decrees and to fear the LORD our God, so that we might always prosper and be kept alive, as is the case today. [25]And if we are careful to obey all this law before the LORD our God, as he has commanded us, that will be our righteousness." (**Deu 6:1-12,20-25**).

At some point in Jewish history the commandment to *"tie them as symbols on your hands"* was taken literally, leading to the development of phylacteries, a pair of small boxes containing passages from Scripture written on parchment. The admonition was probably metaphorical in nature, however, as suggested in **Exodus 13:9**, where Moses refers in a similar way to keeping the Passover. Either way, what is being stressed is *active remembering*. In OT worship simple mental recall is never an end in itself.

Inherent in the act of remembering is passing down the story from generation to generation. This passage suggests that worshiping through remembrance is both taught and modeled by parents.[5] The command to continually repeat the redemption account is framed in an intergenerational context.[6] Today we live in a world where the family is often fragmented. Therefore, the family of God must be intentional about the mingling of generations in worship.

The family of God must be intentional about the mingling of generations in worship.

In **Deuteronomy 26:5-9**, the complete story is told concisely:

> [5]Then you shall declare before the LORD your God: "My father was a wandering Aramean, and he went down into Egypt with a few people and lived there and became a great nation, powerful and numerous. [6]But the Egyptians mistreated **us** and made **us** suffer, putting **us** to hard labor. [7]Then **we** cried out to the LORD, the God of **our** fathers, and the LORD heard **our** voice and saw **our**

---

[5] For practical applications to this concept see **Liesch, 51-66**.
[6] See also **Ex 12:26-27; 13:14-15; Josh 4:21-24; Pss 71:18; 78:3-7; 145:4; Isa 38:19; Nehemiah 8**. For an example of an intentional intergenerational worship gathering, see **Joel 2**.

*misery, toil and oppression. [8]So the L*ORD *brought **us** out of Egypt with a mighty hand and an outstretched arm, with great terror and with miraculous signs and wonders. [9]He brought **us** to this place and gave **us** this land, a land flowing with milk and honey. . . . (emphasis added)*

The corporate nature of this recitation is unmistakable, as indicated by the emphasized pronouns. It is decidedly part of a worship gathering, where the first fruits are being offered at the altar of the Lord. The story of God's merciful and miraculous intervention at the exodus is the story of all Israelites for generations to come. Williams points out, "Each time the affirmation was recited, the worshiper bridged the time and space gap and became identified with that never-to-be-repeated salvation: he or she actualized, contemporized, re-presented history" (**86**).

Remembering in the New Testament

These snapshots of redemptive history provide the basis for creedal statements. A creed is "a brief authoritative formula of religious belief."[7] Biblical creeds are "not precise definitions of doctrinal issues but rather acts of worship in response to God's revelation of himself through deeds of salvation and covenant faithfulness in behalf of His people" (**R. Leonard, "Service,"299**). Using creedal statements in worship is a means of recapping important events into a summary statement, which in turn becomes a vehicle of worship. We have seen this exemplified in the OT; NT worshipers also encapsulated the story of their redemption into brief declarations:

---

[7] Readers aligned with the Christian Church, Nondenominational, will likely be familiar with the slogan "No creed but Christ." This important declaration was a reaction to *human inspired creeds* that were being used as tests of fellowship in the 1800s. Alexander Campbell, in *The Christian System*, "summed up the apostolic faith in certain 'gospel facts' or 'moral facts,' principally the story of Christ's incarnation, death, resurrection, and ascension for our sake." The intent of this discussion is to note that creedal statements are biblical in nature. Therefore extrabiblical creeds, such as the historic Apostles' Creed are outside its scope. It is worth noting, however, that as early as 1832, Campbell endorsed the Apostle's Creed as "a faithful rendition of the 'gospel facts'" (**Blowers, 254**).

Beyond all question, the mystery of godliness is great:
He appeared in a body,
  was vindicated by the Spirit,
was seen by angels,
  was preached among the nations,
was believed on in the world,
  was taken up in glory. (1Tm 3:16)

The above passage appears to be a fragment from an early hymn, identifiable by the similar length and structure of each line. The brief portrait of Christ captures the truth of who He is and at the same time offers praise to Him. Walter Liefeld notes that "it centers on Christ who came to us and the response he has received and deserves to receive further from us. The proclamation of Christ evokes a response" (145).

[3]For what I received I passed on to you as of first impor-tance: that Christ died for our sins according to the Scriptures, [4]that he was buried, that he was raised on the third day according to the Scriptures, [5]and that he appeared to Peter, and then to the Twelve. (1Cor 15:3-5)

This early creed highlights the importance of acknowl-edging the Scriptures as the source of truth, emphasizing the two most important events in all of history, the death and resurrection of Jesus Christ. The historical nature of the pas-sage is also noteworthy. "It was not something which was enacted in another place, like the activities of the Greek gods, but a happening that can be given date and place and per-son" (Chafin, 180). In *verses 6ff*, Paul claims that there are still eyewitnesses to the resurrection, including himself. This is one of many passages that should prompt us to include reg-ularly the resurrection in our Sunday liturgies; without it, the gospel story is incomplete.

[6]Who, being in very nature God,
  did not consider equality with God something to be
  grasped,
[7]but made himself nothing,
  taking the very nature of a servant,
  being made in human likeness.
[8]And being found in appearance as a man,

he humbled himself
and became obedient to death—even death on a cross!
⁹Therefore God exalted him to the highest place
and gave him the name that is above every name,
¹⁰that at the name of Jesus every knee should bow,
in heaven and on earth and under the earth,
¹¹and every tongue confess that Jesus Christ is Lord,
*to the glory of God the Father. (**Php 2:6-11**)*

This exquisite passage is perhaps the best known creedal statement of the NT. Like *1 Timothy 3:16*, it is probably an early Christian hymn, a "marvellous description of Christ's self-humbling in His incarnation and death, together with His subsequent exaltation by God to the place of highest honour" (**O Brien, 187**).[8]

These three examples *show* us how the early Christians worshiped, and should prompt us in the verbalizing that we do in corporate worship. A picture of Jesus—His redemptive work, His victorious resurrection, His imminent return—evokes response that is not dependent upon who *I* am or how *I* feel. It is difficult to be self-absorbed in our worship when Jesus is truly at the center of it.

> ## It is difficult to be self-absorbed in our worship when Jesus is truly at the center of it.

RE-PRESENTATION: ACTIONS SPEAK LOUDER THAN WORDS

J. Gerald Janzen highlights the fact that the biblical narrative "interweaves the events of the exodus with instructions for ritual observances that are to celebrate the exodus" (**97**). Donald L. Williams calls these ritual acts "re-presentation of history," which he points to as the overriding purpose in Israelite worship (**85**). Cultic actions were designed to bring the past into the present. God, who is not bound by time,

---

[8] For a thorough treatment see Ralph Martin, *Carmen Christi: Philippians 2:5-11 in Recent Interpretation and in the Setting of Early Christian Worship* (Grand Rapids: Eerdmans, 1983).

provided a means by which the children of Israel could participate in events that had happened years before, thereby claiming them in their own particular time and space.

Webber explains, "The temple rituals were re-presentations through drama and thus symbolically represented the relationship between God and the worshiper, as in the act of ratification at Mount Sinai. They also looked forward to the final once-for-all sacrifice of Christ when the ultimate and eternal drama of salvation would be carried out in the death and resurrection of Christ" (*Old and New*, 78).

Re-presentation, along with the corporate nature of worship, is made evident by the importance that the OT places on festivals. Walter Brueggemann proposes that the festivals relate to God as both Creator and Redeemer. He describes the festival as "a gesture made in order to refer and relate all of life to the character and action of YHWH, the one who is known in festival as giver and transformer of life" (*Ancient*, 12).

Festivals

One way in which re-presentation took place was through celebrating the Sabbath. Instituted by God (*Ex 20:8-11*) as a day of rest and as a weekly celebration, the Sabbath was a sign of His covenant relationship with Israel and future generations (*Ex 31:12-17*). This festival was a reminder of God's creation: *"For in six days the LORD made the heavens and the earth, the sea, and all that is in them, but he rested on the seventh day"* (*Ex 20:11*), as well as redemption: *"Remember that you were slaves in Egypt and that the LORD your God brought you out of there with a mighty hand and an outstretched arm"* (*Deu 5:15*). There were severe consequences for breaking the Sabbath (*Ex 31:14-15*). Every seventh year was also to be observed as a Sabbath year, in which the land was to rest from planting (*Lev 25:4-5*).

Another manner of re-presentation was through three major agricultural festivals (*Ex 23:14-17*): Unleavened Bread (Passover) (*Num 28:16-25; Deu 16:1-8*), Harvest (Firstfruits,

Chapter 2
God the Redeemer

67

Weeks, or Pentecost) (*Ex 34:22; Num 28:26-31*), and Ingathering (Tabernacles or Booths) (*Ex 34:22; Lev 23:34,39-43; Deu 16:13; Num 29:12-38*). It was no accident that these festivals were related to nature as they were a means of redeeming the pagan practices of divinizing nature. The festivals reminded Israel that nature was a channel of blessing from God, not an object of worship. The fruit of the land could, however, be used to worship Him.

Three times a year all adult males were called to worship at the tabernacle (and later the temple) as a reminder of God's provision and care for His children. Characteristic of these gatherings were praise, joy, sacrifice, repentance and remembrance. The festivals were punctuated by full participation of the worshipers, including the offering of incense, tithing, purification

> **God wants heartfelt and sincere observances, not outward ceremonies alone.**

rites, music, dance, and drama. Seven major festivals were being observed by the time of the NT, each connected with historical events in the history of Israel.[9] God expected these observances to be heartfelt and sincere. Outward ceremonies alone did not please Him.

The celebration of Passover exemplifies both re-presenting and passing down the story. Godfrey Ashby describes it as "a *family* event celebrating and actualizing God's mighty redemptive act in history" (53). There is a hopeful expectancy about this night. When the youngest son asks, "Why is this night different from all other nights?" the story is retold. But rather than being a completely cerebral event where remembering is merely an exercise in thinking, dramatic actions utilizing touch, taste, and smell bring the memories to life. Parsley dipped in salt-water recalls the tears of the

[9] For further study see **Hill**, 121-125. In addition to the three festivals listed are the Feast of Trumpets (Rosh Hashanah) and the Day of Atonement (Yom Kippur), which are biblical feasts (see *Leviticus 23*). The Feast of Purim, and Feast of Lights (Hanukkah) were developed later in Israel's history.

slaves; the shank bone is symbolic of the sacrificial lamb; bitter herbs reflect the affliction of slavery; four glasses of wine represent four stages of the exodus.

> This memorable celebration has retained its value for our days as in days of old, and has exercised a great pedagogical influence upon the children for which purpose it was chiefly instituted. . . . The story tells of suffering, of sorrow and pain, of struggle with the iron yoke of slavery, of afflictions which penetrate to the very core of life; it also speaks of hope for deliverance and of idealistic devotion to the cause of humanity as evinced by the illustrious leader, Moses, who created a free people out of slaves and gave them laws of the highest ethical value. On the occasion of this celebration every Jewish home receives the atmosphere of a sanctuary in which each member of the family is a priest and the housemaster—the high priest—a sanctuary to serve the purest human ideals and the living God (**Idelsohn, 173**).[10]

New Testament Re-Presentation

The centrality of redemption extends to the worship of the NT because of Christ's once-and-for-all sacrifice. Placing redemption at the center of our gatherings results in a form of response that Webber defines as enactment, or re-telling and acting out a story

> **By enacting the story, we have a more meaningful encounter with God.**

(*Old and New*, 73). By enacting, rather than merely sitting and listening to the story, we can have a more meaningful encounter with the God who redeemed us.

The Lord's Supper

In the NT, the drama of redemption is encompassed in symbols that re-present the gospel story. The Lord's Supper was initiated within the context of the Passover, and is the

---

[10] The ritual described here was developed long after the OT, and quite possibly the NT period. As long as the temple was standing, the OT Passover ritual was followed.

most palpable example of enactment in the context of the NT. This meal brings the past into the present, framing remembrance in a new light.

It is helpful to understand that there is a difference between the ancient and contemporary perceptions of memory. John Koenig states that in the Jewish mind "events of the past are re-presented through ritual in a very palpable manner" (65). In

> **The Lord's Supper brings the past into the present, framing remembrance in a new light.**

his discussion of the *eleventh chapter of 1 Corinthians*, Laurence Stookey masterfully places this matter in context:

> For most twentieth-century Christians, remembering is a solitary experience involving mental recall. But for ancient Jews and early Christians (the first of whom were all Jews), remembrance was a corporate act in which the event remembered was experienced anew through ritual repetition. To remember was to do something, not to think about something. Thus in *verse 25*, the words 'do this' are even more crucial than 'in remembrance of me.' Almost universally we 'do this,' but often we suppose that in doing it, we are primarily to 'think about this.' We have become passive and cerebral, often thinking primarily about the historical ministry of Jesus. But the intention of Paul is that we actively participate—and in the participation experience anew for ourselves the presence of the living Christ among us. (**28-29**)

The Greek word *anamnesis*[11] is helpful in analyzing the mind-set of the early Christians. Kenny Boles, Ozark Christian College Greek professor, defines the word as "bringing something up into the conscience now; to do again." He agrees that merely remembering is a weak translation, suggesting that partaking of the emblems brings Jesus into our midst more than a routine get-together.[12] This kind of remembrance allows us to *participate* in the death and resurrection of Christ,

[11] Translated, "remembrance." See *Lk 22:19; 1Cor 11:24,25; Heb 10:3*.
[12] Kenny Boles, Interview by author, 7 October 2002, Joplin, Missouri, Ozark Christian College.

not simply to *think* about long ago events. It is the Holy Spirit who accomplishes this active remembering.

Mark Moore asserts that in the Supper we not only remember backward, but also forward (to Jesus' return), inward (to examine ourselves), and outward (to pro-

> **It is the Holy Spirit who accomplishes this active remembering.**

claim unity). He observes, "It is indeed a wondrous mystery that such a fragile memorial, comprised of such common and transitory elements, has endured so tenaciously the ravages of time" (226). Yet, perhaps because of our modern understanding of memory, we frequently celebrate this observance with little joy, reverence, or even importance. We need to find a way to "remember" that recalls *all* of the significance of the redemptive work of Jesus Christ.

Baptism

Baptism is a powerful symbol that reenacts the death, burial, and resurrection of Jesus. Each time we witness a baptism, we visualize dying to sin and beginning a new life.

> [3] *Or don't you know that all of us who were baptized into Christ Jesus were baptized into his death?* [4] *We were therefore buried with him through baptism into death in order that, just as Christ was raised from the dead through the glory of the Father, we too may live a new life.* (**Rom 6:3-4**)

Jack Cottrell sheds light on what happens during this act of surrender:

> When we became united with Christ's death in baptism, our old sinful self was put to death—not by our own will power, but by the power of his holy cross. It is as if, in his death, Jesus became a flame that is capable of extinguishing everything having to do with sin and death. When we are baptized into his death (buried with him in baptism), we touch this flame; and it consumes the "old man" of sin, and sets us ablaze with a holy fire that continues to purge the residual sin from our lives. (*Romans*, **1:385**)

Like the Lord's Supper, baptism is not reducible to a one-time event. It is often ignored as a liturgical act, with emphasis given to one individual. But we should consistently remind the church body that one life impacts all, and that the result of our own baptism is daily infusing our lives with Holy-Spirit-inspired power for a joyous Christian life.

> **The result of our own baptism is daily infusing our lives with Holy-Spirit-inspired power.**

COMMUNAL RECITAL: JOYOUS CELEBRATION

As we have already noted, the Bible emphasizes the communal nature of worship, "the corporate action of the community in response to God's acts of grace in history" (**Beachy, 9**).

> I will declare your name to my brothers;
>   in the congregation[13] I will praise you. (**Ps 22:22**)

> David praised the LORD in the presence of the whole assembly, saying,
>   "Praise be to you, O LORD,
>   God of our father Israel,
>   from everlasting to everlasting. (**1Chr 29:10**)

These corporate gatherings often occurred in the midst of celebration. For example, at the return of the Ark of the Covenant from its capture by the Philistines, David's praise included this lengthy discourse that conveyed the story of God's redemptive purposes:

> [8]Give thanks to the LORD, call on his name;
>   make known among the nations what he has done.
> [9]Sing to him, sing praise to him;
>   tell of all his wonderful acts.
> [10]Glory in his holy name;
>   let the hearts of those who seek the LORD rejoice.
> [11]Look to the LORD and his strength;
>   seek his face always.

---

[13] *Qahal*, also translated "assembly," "company," or "multitude." See also **2Chr 6:13; Neh 8:2; Pss 35:18; 107:32; Joel 2:16**. The term can refer both to a general assembly or a group gathered for worship, war, or political purposes.

¹²Remember the wonders he has done,
  his miracles, and the judgments he pronounced,
¹³O descendants of Israel his servant,
  O sons of Jacob, his chosen ones.
¹⁴He is the LORD our God;
  his judgments are in all the earth.
¹⁵He remembers his covenant forever,
  the word he commanded, for a thousand generations,
¹⁶the covenant he made with Abraham,
  the oath he swore to Isaac.
¹⁷He confirmed it to Jacob as a decree,
  to Israel as an everlasting covenant:
¹⁸"To you I will give the land of Canaan
  as the portion you will inherit."
¹⁹When they were but few in number,
  few indeed, and strangers in it,
²⁰they wandered from nation to nation,
  from one kingdom to another.
²¹He allowed no man to oppress them;
  for their sake he rebuked kings:
²²"Do not touch my anointed ones;
  do my prophets no harm."
²³Sing to the LORD, all the earth;
  proclaim his salvation day after day.
²⁴Declare his glory among the nations,
  his marvelous deeds among all peoples.
²⁵For great is the LORD and most worthy of praise;
  he is to be feared above all gods.
²⁶For all the gods of the nations are idols,
  but the LORD made the heavens.
²⁷Splendor and majesty are before him;
  strength and joy in his dwelling place.
²⁸Ascribe to the LORD, O families of nations,
  ascribe to the LORD glory and strength,
²⁹ascribe to the LORD the glory due his name.
Bring an offering and come before him;
  worship the LORD in the splendor of his holiness.
³⁰Tremble before him, all the earth!
  The world is firmly established; it cannot be moved.
³¹Let the heavens rejoice, let the earth be glad;
  let them say among the nations, "The LORD reigns!"
³²Let the sea resound, and all that is in it;
  let the fields be jubilant, and everything in them!
³³Then the trees of the forest will sing,
  they will sing for joy before the LORD,

for he comes to judge the earth.
[34]*Give thanks to the L*ORD*, for he is good;*
  his love endures forever.
[35]*Cry out, "Save us, O God our Savior;*
  gather us and deliver us from the nations,
that we may give thanks to your holy name,
  that we may glory in your praise."
[36]*Praise be to the L*ORD*, the God of Israel,*
  from everlasting to everlasting.

*Then all the people said "Amen" and "Praise the L*ORD*."*
*(**1Chr 16:8-36**)*[14]

Note that remembering is at the center of this pro-
nouncement (*v. 12*), which is nearly identical to *Psalms 105,
96, and 106*.[15] It is not just the Israelites who remember; their
praise is possible because God remembered them first and

> **It is not just the Israelites
> who remember; their
> praise is possible because
> God remembered them.**

forever.[16] Moreover, the sec-
tion quoted from *Psalm 96*
places emphasis on recognizing God as Creator, which we
have previously recognized as
a basis for response. The con-
nection between these two passages gives valuable insight
into what David deemed important for the heart of corporate worship.

Followers of Christ are often found gathered together in
the NT.[17] The writer of Hebrews admonishes, *"Let us not give
up meeting together, as some are in the habit of doing, but let us
encourage one another—and all the more as you see the Day
approaching"* (*Heb 10:25*). It must be emphasized that these
gatherings in no way suggest an order or style of worship. As
a matter of fact, the concept of a "worship service" is con-
spicuously absent from the NT. Ritualizing worship in a par-

---

[14] This important event also marks the transition of Levitical duties from trans-
porting the tabernacle to music ministry, taking a role as "worship leaders."
  [15] *Vv. 8-22 = Ps 105:1-15; vv. 23-33 = Ps 96:1-13; vv. 34-36 = Ps 106:1,47,48.*
  [16] When God remembers, something happens! See *Gen 8:1; 30:22.*
  [17] *Acts 1:14; 2:1,44,46; 5:12; 14:27; 15:30; 1Cor 11:18,20,33,34.* The gathered
church will be discussed in ch. 4.

ticular manner is Jewish in nature, and the sacrificial system was rendered unnecessary at the death and resurrection of Jesus. It should not be inferred, however, that celebration was missing from the hearts of the early church! The story of redemption through the work of Jesus Christ was surely recounted again and again with joyous remembrance and anticipation.

THE SONG OF THE REDEEMED: REVELATION

Revelation is not without recitations as acts of worship. *Revelation 15*, for example, portrays worshipers singing the song of Moses:

> *Great and marvelous are your deeds,*
>   *Lord God Almighty.*
> *Just and true are your ways,*
>   *King of the ages.*
> *4Who will not fear you, O Lord,*
>   *and bring glory to your name?*
> *For you alone are holy.*
> *All nations will come*
>   *and worship before you,*
> *for your righteous acts have been revealed.*
>   (*Rev 15:3b-4*)[18]

We have already seen that *Revelation 4* reinforces the honoring of God as Creator. The homage paid, however, is not only to God, but also to His Son. William Hendrickson points to the victorious work of Christ as a primary reason for this:

> Throughout the prophecies of this wonderful book the Christ is ever pictured as the Victor, the Conqueror. . . . He conquers death, Hades, the *dragon*, the beast, the false prophet, the men who worship the beast, etc. *He* is victorious; hence, so are *we*! Even when we seem to be hopelessly defeated. (**13**)

[18] Some commentators believe this to refer to *Exodus 15*, while others align it with *Deuteronomy 32*. Either way, the similarity to the recitations of the OT is valid.

Chapter 2
God the Redeemer

The worship of *Revelation 5* is devoted to worship of the Lamb, the most common image for Jesus in the letter:

> [12]*In a loud voice they sang:*
>> *"Worthy is the Lamb, who was slain*
>> *to receive power and wealth and wisdom and strength*
>> *and honor and glory and praise!"*
>
> [13]*Then I heard every creature in heaven and on earth and under the earth and on the sea, and all that is in them, singing:*
>> *"To him who sits on the throne and to the Lamb*
>> *be praise and honor and glory and power,*
>>> *for ever and ever!"*
>
> [14]*The four living creatures said, "Amen," and the elders fell down and worshiped.* (**Rev 5:12-14**)

The redemptive work of Jesus is in view here, just as God's redemptive work was at the center of the worship of Israel. This recitation is particularly poignant, as the writer had *"wept and wept because no one was found who was worthy to open the scroll or look inside"* (**Rev 5:4**). Out of weeping, though, comes joy unspeakable!

> [9]*And they sang a new song:*
>> *"You are worthy to take the scroll*
>>> *and to open its seals,*
>> *because you were slain,*
>>> *and with your blood you purchased men for God*
>>> *from every tribe and language and people and*
>>> *nation.*
>> [10]*You have made them to be a kingdom and priests to*
>>> *serve our God,*
>> *and they will reign on the earth."* (**Rev 5:9-10**)

Revelation 14 features the song of the redeemed:

> [1]*Then I looked, and there before me was the Lamb, standing on Mount Zion, and with him 144,000 who had his name and his Father's name written on their foreheads.* [2]*And I heard a sound from heaven like the roar of rushing waters and like a loud peal of thunder. The sound I heard was like that of harpists playing their harps.* [3]*And they sang a new song before the throne and before the four living creatures and the elders. No one could learn the song except the 144,000 who had been*

*redeemed from the earth. 4These are those who did not defile themselves with women, for they kept themselves pure. They follow the Lamb wherever he goes. They were purchased from among men and offered as first-fruits to God and the Lamb. (**Rev 14:1-4**)*

The "new song" language found in Revelation is also found in the Psalms:

> *Sing to the LORD a new song,*
> *for he has done marvelous things;*
> *his right hand and his holy arm*
> *have worked salvation for him. (**Ps 98:1**)[19]*

In both contexts, the song is related to redemption. It is not so much "new" because it has never been heard before, as because it is related to the newness of life that comes from redemption. That is not to say that we should not be singing newly written songs, but

> **We can look forward to a much greater breadth and depth of music in the presence of God and the Lamb.**

that older songs can still carry the same message. We can look forward to breadth and depth of music in heaven that we will never be able to experience here on earth because we will be in the presence of God and the Lamb.

CONCLUSION

We have seen that redemption was central to the worship life of ancient Israel. The response to that all-important act of Yahweh was to reenact and recite the story again and again. It was not just *thinking*, but also *doing*. The early Christians, Jews who had been brought up in that atmosphere, continued to recite and reenact as they remembered the ultimate act of redemption: the life, death, and resurrection of Jesus Christ. As the church awaits His return, we can be certain that the Redeemer, the Lamb of God, who has taken away the sins of the world, is surrounded by worship

Chapter 2
God the Redeemer

as He sits at the right hand of the Father. In the meantime, we do our best to recite and reenact the gospel story through the Lord's Supper, baptism, preaching, reciting Scripture, praying together, and singing the song of the redeemed.

What Do You Say?

1. Do you think Christians today are open to recitation as a vehicle of worship? How might this be accomplished in a "traditional" setting? In a "contemporary" setting?

2. For many, reenactment is a new concept in gathered worship. Describe your own understanding of this biblical act. Through what vehicles does your particular body of believers already reenact the gospel story? What else might you do to recover this practice?

3. What is the central thought expressed at the Lord's Supper in your context? What have you learned from this chapter that might enhance or add to this concept?

4. There are no biblical examples of generations being separated for the purposes of gathered worship. Why do you think this is so? What implications does this fact have for today?

"*Christian worship is the most momentous, the most urgent, the most glorious action that can take place in human life.*"

—Karl Barth

"*Wash your face every morning in a bath of praise.*"

—Charles Spurgeon

A
Wedding

We do not talk much today about covenants. When my friend asked me to give a Communion meditation at her wedding, I began to explore the relationship between weddings and covenant. This is the result.

Genilyn and Adam have chosen, on this day that is all about them, to invite us to share in something that is not all about them. I find this to be admirable, and a good precursor of who will be at the center of their lives together.

This meal, of which we are all about to partake, and this ceremony we have gathered to witness, have a lot in common.

They are both about a bride and groom.

They are both about memory—old memories and new ones being made.

They are both about community—about sharing together in an important and life-changing event.

And, most importantly I think, they are about a covenant. Promises made and promises kept. Many promises have already been kept today; the vows that Genilyn and Adam make are forming a new covenant, promises to be kept for the rest of their lives.

The Israelites made vows too, about such things as love, honor, and obedience. But they could not keep their promises. That covenant was broken, over and over.

Which brings us to this Table. On the night He was betrayed, Jesus took the bread, and after He had given thanks, broke it, saying, "This is my body which is for you; do this in remembrance of me." And in the same manner He took the cup, saying, "This is the blood of my New Covenant; as often as you drink it, remember me."

This "New Covenant" is like no other, before or since. Because Jesus Christ paid so high a price that even when we break it, He does not.

And so we eat, His radiant Bride, anticipating His return. We remember, the only Once and For All Sacrifice ever to be given. We share, with joy and thanksgiving, knowing that while this particular group of people will likely never be gathered again, when we separate and partake on any given Sunday, we will still do so in concert. And we renew our vows to our Lord Jesus Christ, to love, honor, and obey.

CHAPTER THREE

GOD, THE COVENANT MAKER

I will establish my covenant as an everlasting covenant
between me and you and your descendants after you
for the generations to come, to be your God
and the God of your descendants after you.
Genesis 17:7

God showed His love for His people in the saving events of the Passover, in the rescue from Egypt, in the passage through the Red Sea, but above all in the covenant, when the people bound themselves to God who is ever faithful to His promises. (**Crichton, 10**)

THE SIGNIFICANCE OF COVENANT

Worship and covenant, characteristic of a community of believers, are not possible apart from each other. Worship, as expressed in cultic rituals, is empty and pointless when separated from a relationship with the covenant-making God.

Covenants, simply put, are built upon promises made and promises kept. The history of Israel is permeated with the promises of Yahweh. The great patriarch, Abraham, for example, is assured that his people will become a mighty nation (*Gen 12:2-3*).[1] Ralph Martin asserts that "the fulfillment of these promises

[1] Andrew Hill notes that Abram's first act of worship, or response to God's revelation, was obedience: *"So Abram left"* (*Gen 12:4*). See Hill, 32.

Covenants are built upon promises made and promises kept.

becomes the impetus for the people's response of worship" (**"Patriarchal,"** 95). God uses the ancient practice of covenant to secure a relationship between Himself and Israel.

Janice Leonard notes that the covenant between God and His people "regulates worship and provides much of its structure, rationale, and vocabulary" (**"Concept,"** 56). The ancients were familiar with covenants as political treaties, in which the "lord" and his "servant" entered into an agreement. In return for protection, the "servant" offered his allegiance to his "lord." According to Leonard, covenant "provides the basis for, and is the essence of, the relationship between the Lord God and His people. Through its framework they learn His ways, pledge their allegiance to Him, and respond to Him in worship" (**ibid., 56**). Responding to the Covenant maker acknowledges His lordship over all of life.

Covenants in ancient times were a means of maintaining a relationship between lord and servant without the use of force. This type of agreement was sometimes referred to as a "vassal" or "suzerainty" treaty, because it was made between suzerains, or feudal lords, and their vassals, or servants.[2] The details of

Responding to the Covenant maker acknowledges His lordship over all of life.

the relationship between ancient political covenants and the covenants of the Old, and ultimately the New, Testaments provide a fascinating study. In summary, covenants consisted of the following:

❖ Preamble and Historical prologue (the king identifies himself, stating his names and titles, accomplishments; one or both relate the history of the relationship)

---

[2] Covenants were also made between individuals, such as Jacob and Laban (**Gen 31:44-54**) or Jonathan and David (**1Sa 18:3**), or states or political units, such as Abraham and Abimelech (**Gen 21:22-32**) or Hiram and Solomon (**1Kgs 5:12**). These treaties were considered to be made between equals, rather than a servant/lord relationship.

- ❖ Granting of territory
- ❖ Conditions (stipulations)
- ❖ Sanctions (blessings or curses)
- ❖ Oath (swears loyalty)
- ❖ Witnesses (listen and enforce)
- ❖ Sign (verifies the existence)
- ❖ Provision for a permanent record and public reading of the text at periodical intervals (a covenant was not considered in existence until it was written, sealed, and delivered to the servant king)
- ❖ Ceremony (sacrifice, sharing of coat or weapons, meal)

It is not difficult to see the relationship between these elements and the covenant established between Yahweh and the children of Israel. God often identifies Himself and His right to lordship, as in **Exodus 20:1**, *"I am the LORD your God, who brought you out of Egypt, out of the land of slavery."* (See also **Deu 1:1-5; Josh 24:1-2**.) Canaan, the Promised Land, is the territory; the Ten Commandments give the conditions; Leviticus and Numbers outline the sanctions. Oaths, witnesses, circumcision (a sign), public readings, meals, sacrifices—all can be found in the worship practices of the Israelite community. The Book of Deuteronomy is a covenant document; its entire structure fits the covenant practices outlined above.[3]

At the core of the covenantal relationship is this promise from Yahweh: *"I will walk among you and be your God, and you will be my people"* (**Lev 26:12**). This declaration establishes a requirement of exclusivity: the children of Israel have been chosen by the one and only Creator, and are to be obedient and loyal only to Him. God's loyalty to His people is characterized by *chesed*, His covenant love. This term is difficult to convey with any particular English word. Divine *chesed* saves people from disaster or oppression, sustains life, and counteracts God's wrath; it is eternal and unfailing (**Baer, 211-218**). It is undeserved, yet freely given.

[3] For a comprehensive examination of ancient covenants see **J.F. Leonard, *I Will Be Their God: Understanding the Covenant*** (Chicago: Laudemont Press, 1992).

The worship of Israel is inextricably linked to covenant. Walter Brueggemann deftly summarizes:

> It is right to say, then, that Israel's worship is to be understood as a *practice of covenant* whereby Israel variously receives and affirms the covenant, maintains and sustains the covenant, and takes steps to renew and revivify the covenant when it has been violated. It does so by various acts of gratitude and obedience, by gestures of submission and loyalty, and by words of affirmation and praise. Worship consists in words and gestures by which Israel regularly resituates its life in the ongoing narrative of YHWH who creates, judges, and rescues. (**Ancient, 8**)

God had made a covenant with Abraham (**Gen 17:1-14**), Jacob, and Isaac (**Ex 2:24; Lev 26:42**). He had established a memorable covenant with Noah (**Gen 9:8-17**). During this era corporate worship had been seen primarily within the confines of family, with the patriarchs serving as priests.[4] The building of altars was often at the center of these acts of worship.[5] After the Israelites are rescued from Egypt, however, at the foot of Mt. Sinai, a pattern of corporate worship begins to emerge.

> **The worship of Israel is inextricably linked to covenant.**

EXODUS 24

The twenty-fourth chapter of Exodus records the response of Israel to the overtures of Yahweh. Moses has been on Mt. Sinai receiving the laws that God has set before His people. Exodus 24 provides a description of the actual rites surrounding the ratification of a covenant. The law is read; the people respond and make sacrifice, seal the covenant with an oath, and participate in a covenant meal. This amazing encounter between God and His children offers some important insights into what God expects from a gathering of worshipers.

---

[4] A notable exception is Moses and Miriam leading in praise after the crossing of the Red Sea (**Ex 15:1-21**).

[5] Abraham was a prolific altar builder; see **Gen 12:8; 13:18; 22:9**. Altars were identified with sacrifice, prayer, and calling on the Name of the Lord.

¹Then he said to Moses, "Come up to the LORD, you and Aaron, Nadab and Abihu, and seventy of the elders of Israel. You are to worship at a distance, ²but Moses alone is to approach the LORD; the others must not come near. And the people may not come up with him."

³When Moses went and told the people all the LORD's words and laws, they responded with one voice, "Everything the LORD has said we will do." ⁴Moses then wrote down everything the LORD had said.

He got up early the next morning and built an altar at the foot of the mountain and set up twelve stone pillars representing the twelve tribes of Israel. ⁵Then he sent young Israelite men, and they offered burnt offerings and sacrificed young bulls as fellowship offerings to the LORD. ⁶Moses took half of the blood and put it in bowls, and the other half he sprinkled on the altar. ⁷Then he took the Book of the Covenant and read it to the people. They responded, "We will do everything the LORD has said; we will obey."

⁸Moses then took the blood, sprinkled it on the people and said, "This is the blood of the covenant that the LORD has made with you in accordance with all these words."

⁹Moses and Aaron, Nadab and Abihu, and the seventy elders of Israel went up ¹⁰and saw the God of Israel. Under his feet was something like a pavement made of sapphire, clear as the sky itself. ¹¹But God did not raise his hand against these leaders of the Israelites; they saw God, and they ate and drank. **(Ex 24:1-11)**

Arthur Pink describes this gathering as "a scene for which there is nothing approaching a parallel on all the pages of inspired history prior to the Divine Incarnation and the tabernacling of God among men. It might suitably be designated the Old Testament Mount of Transfiguration, for here Jehovah manifested His glory as never before or after during the whole of the Mosaic economy" **(175)**. At this meeting, God not only ratified the ancient covenant He had made with Abraham, He inaugurated a new era in the worship life of His chosen people.

The call from God to worship is a critical ingredient in this passage: *"Then He said to Moses, 'Come up to the LORD, you and Aaron, Nadab and Abihu, and seventy of the elders of Israel. You are to worship at a distance, but Moses alone is to approach the LORD; the others must not come near"* (*Ex 24: 1-2*). The meeting here is on God's terms, not the terms of men.

The Word

The worship gathering in *Exodus 24* included the reading of God's Word and a meal of fellowship in the presence of God (*Ex 24:7,11*). In essence, these elements form liturgical actions, foreshadowing the emphasis that the church universal would place on Word and Table.[6] Placing these elements at the heart of Sunday gatherings today ensures a consistent, ongoing renewal of our covenantal relationship with God.

"For both the Old and New Testaments, one consistent pillar of true worship has been the Word of God," insists Timothy Ralston (**196**). Indeed, the Israelites' declaration, *"We will do everything the LORD has said; we will obey"* (*Ex 24:7*), is a response to the reading of the Book of the Covenant. Whether this book was the Decalogue only, or included the laws God had laid down directly preceding this encounter, it is clear that it was a direct word from Yahweh. From this point on, the Word is prominent in the corporate gatherings of Israel.

The Psalmist found delight in the Word: *"Oh, how I love your law! I meditate on it all day long"* (*Ps 119:87*). The entirety of *Psalm 119* is a testimony to the power and beauty of God's law. The Hebrew word, *torah*, is variously translated, "law," "promise," "word," "decrees," "commands," and "precepts," among others. Walter Zorn ascertains, "The aim of the author, without question, is to glorify God for the gift of His instructions for life" (**376**). Reading the Word is paramount in worship, both public and

> **Reading the Word is paramount in worship, both public and private.**

---

[6] Early in the church's history, Word (both Sermons and Scripture Readings) and Table (the celebration of the Lord's Supper) became the center of Sunday gatherings.

private. Doing so is both an *act of worship*, and a *means of instruction*.

A striking example of love for the Word of God is found in Nehemiah 8:

> When the seventh month came and the Israelites had settled in their towns, ¹all the people assembled as one man in the square before the Water Gate. They told Ezra the scribe to bring out the Book of the Law of Moses, which the LORD had commanded for Israel.
>
> ²So on the first day of the seventh month Ezra the priest brought the Law before the assembly, which was made up of men and women and all who were able to understand. ³He read it aloud from daybreak till noon as he faced the square before the Water Gate in the presence of the men, women and others who could understand. And all the people listened attentively to the Book of the Law.
>
> ⁴Ezra the scribe stood on a high wooden platform built for the occasion. Beside him on his right stood Mattithiah, Shema, Anaiah, Uriah, Hilkiah and Maaseiah; and on his left were Pedaiah, Mishael, Malkijah, Hashum, Hashbaddanah, Zechariah and Meshullam.
>
> ⁵Ezra opened the book. All the people could see him because he was standing above them; and as he opened it, the people all stood up. ⁶Ezra praised the LORD, the great God; and all the people lifted their hands and responded, "Amen! Amen!" Then they bowed down and worshiped the LORD with their faces to the ground. (**Neh 8:1-6**)

This remarkable scene takes place after the Israelites had returned from the Babylonian exile,[7] in the setting of a festival[8] and covenant renewal. Nehemiah had completed the restoration of the temple, a considerable achievement, but it was the Book of the Law that the returnees longed to see and hear. The

---

[7] In 587 BC, Jerusalem fell to the Babylonians; there is disagreement concerning the manner in which the Jews practiced worship during this time. It is probable though that, due to the impossibility of sacrificial worship, a more individualistic type developed including confessions, laments, prayer, and singing (see **Psalm 137**). Ezra and Nehemiah were instrumental in the reestablishment of Israel's faith and worship practices.

[8] The first day of the seventh month was the Feast of Trumpets (**Lev 23:24**).

people themselves requested that Ezra bring the book before them and responded with attentiveness, respect, and worship. It was apparently an intergenerational group, as it included all who could understand. The actions described—standing, lifting hands, crying "Amen," and bowing prostrate—were typical of Hebrew worship. The text makes it obvious that they worshiped Yahweh, not the book itself, but there is no doubt that the Word was held in high esteem, a reaction that we would do well to emulate in some way.

To hear a word from God today requires the reading of Scripture. In fact, insists John Stott, "Word and worship belong indissolubly to each other. All worship is an intelligent and loving response to the revelation of God, because it is the adoration of His Name" (82). Stott continues to argue for the necessity of preaching, which is certainly valid and appropriate. But we must also hold the reading of the Word alone in high esteem. It is impossible to engage in the story without hearing and assimilating it.

> **There is no doubt the Word was held in high esteem, and we would do well to emulate this.**

> So it is not for nothing that Christians continue to emphasize the importance of orality by reading the Bible aloud, and hearing it together, in our worship. By such an act we not only communicate anew our story but indeed participate in that story by ways peculiar to us — peculiar to the people of God who risks embodiment, who works through the timely and the local. By hearing words read aloud we indicate in deed that the Word cannot show its power without our communal listening and obedience. It cannot live without being spoken and heard, always and again spoken to and heard by specific people, with their unique problems and dreams. When the church remembers it is an oral culture it necessarily remembers that the message of the gospel is inseparable from the speakers and doers of the gospel. (**Clapp, 136**)

The NT also gives precedence to the importance of the Word in worship. It is one of the hallmarks of early Christian gatherings, as seen in the book of Acts, which will be discussed further in Chapter 4.

The Table

The importance of meals would also carry over into the New Testament. In *At the Origins of Christian Worship*, Larry Hurtado stresses significance of meals, not only to Jews, but also to other religious groups. He points out that "religious meals expressed group solidarity in the religion, memorialised great events in Jewish religious history, and were festive, celebratory affairs" (34). Since the event at Mt. Sinai in *Exodus 24* was the ratification of a covenant, the sharing of a meal was a typical component. Samuel Balentine explains that at this meal those assembled were granted "an unparalleled intimacy with the presence of God" (135). The celebration of a meal, the Eucharist, equally important in Christian worship, has its roots here. Jesus' use of a meal to invoke a new covenant prior to His once-and-for-all act of atonement that would ensure access to the Father was full of significance for the Jewish Christians.

Our culture today has a less important view of meals than did the Israelites. Although meals are still universally a time to gather, share, and celebrate, they carried a much deeper meaning at the time of Jesus. Moore asserts that "for the Jews, eating together was a sacred event" (223). Stookey notes that Jesus did not "start from scratch" at the Last Supper, but rather built upon the many times He had previously dined with His disciples (35). He says, "What Jesus did by His death and resurrection was to give far deeper meaning both to this final meal and His earlier meals, so that the church's meal could be seen as nothing other than a Christian Passover feast—a celebration of escape from servitude and death" (35). Koenig concludes that for the early Christians "virtually every meal in those early days was permeated by Jesus' presence" (65).

It seems likely then, that those who had eaten with Jesus

on many occasions expected Him to be present at the Lord's Supper. William Robinson, a Restoration Movement leader of the early twentieth century, "holds that the Lord is not just *remembered* in the communion, He is *present.*" (**Lambert, 13**). Preferring the term, "Real Action," he stressed that Christ is not physically present in the elements, but in the actual taking of the elements—the communing itself (**ibid., 15**).

MINISTERING TO THE SENSES—SYMBOL

Janzen calls attention to another aspect of *Exodus 24*: "The covenant ceremony is rich in a meaning partly spoken and partly acted out. The words give the actions their focus and clarity of meaning; the actions give the words a depth and range of meaning that words can only hint at" (**186**). In this encounter, where God assembles His people for worship, He relies not only on the written or spoken word, but on symbolism as well. The building of an altar, the burnt and fellowship offerings, the sprinkling of the blood, and the sharing of the meal were visible and tactile expressions that allowed the worshipers not only to listen, but to take part. This embrace of the symbolic in worship precedes the building of the tabernacle, which we have seen was replete with symbolism.

Our twenty-first-century minds do not wrap around the concept of symbolism as easily as did those of the ancients. A.S. Herbert explains it well:

> **Our minds do not wrap around the concept of symbolism as easily as did those of the ancients.**

A worshipping community necessarily engages in certain recognized and 'formal' actions. But the actions are something more than a conventional expression or visible illustration of thought. They are thought of as effectively conveying something from man to God, and mediating the divine blessing to man. If we think of them as 'symbolic acts', they are effective in their symbolism, not merely in the sense of stimulating a worshipful attitude, but as necessary to man's worship. They possess intrinsic power to fulfill that which they symbolize. (15)

The significance of symbolism also affects our understanding of the New Covenant meal. "Symbols are real, present, in front of us. But symbols also evoke something beyond the reality in front of us; they evoke something unique in each of us. Bread and wine are symbols of Christ—what He did, what He is doing and what He will do. But they are more than that. They represent a longing in us for communion with divine reality" (64).

COVENANT KEEPING— OBEDIENCE

As God's chosen people, the nation of Israel was set apart to reflect His holiness: *"I am the LORD who brought you up out of Egypt to be your God; therefore be holy, because I am holy"* (*Lev 11:45*). Thus, worship is covenant keeping manifested in worshipers who continually seek to obey and honor God in daily activities. As Ronald Manahan concludes, "Worship and life are intertwined" (71).

> **Worship is covenant keeping by those who seek daily to obey and honor God.**

Because of the Covenant, notes Beachy, "Yahweh's people are not to confine their worship to the limits of the temple or the sacred place, *but rather to recognize Yahweh's lordship over the totality of Israel's life"* (12). Obedience in all things is expected by a covenant-making God. The responses, *"Everything the LORD has said we will do"* (*Ex 24:3*) and *"We will do everything the LORD has said; we will obey"*[9] (*Ex 24:7*), were unified and

---

[9] The Hebrew word, *shama'* translates "obey," "hear," or "listen to." Gören Larsson points out the symmetry between this verse and *Ex 19:5*, where God commands the Israelites to *"obey me fully and keep my covenant."* God expects both hearing and doing (189-190).

emphatic. Of course, eight chapters later these same respondents were dancing around a golden calf, but that does not negate the sincerity of their intentions. It does bring to light the fact that the old covenant had to be continually renewed, and that there are consequences for breaking the covenant (*Exodus 32–34*).

Sometimes the covenant was not broken, but was nevertheless renewed, or ratified.[10] Such is the case in *Joshua 23–24* when the tribes are gathered at the end of Joshua's leadership. The elements of covenant making that were discussed earlier are involved in this meeting. It begins with a recitation of God's saving intervention (*Josh 24:2-13*). Also present are stipulations (*vv. 14-25*), curses, blessings, (*v. 20*) and witnesses (*vv. 22,27*). What is striking about this covenant ceremony is the depth and breadth of obedient response.

> [14]"Now fear the LORD and serve ['abad] him with all faithfulness. Throw away the gods your forefathers worshiped beyond the River and in Egypt, and serve the LORD. [15]But if serving the LORD seems undesirable to you, then choose for yourselves this day whom you will serve, whether the gods your forefathers served beyond the River, or the gods of the Amorites, in whose land you are living. But as for me and my household, we will serve the LORD."
>
> [16]Then the people answered, "Far be it from us to forsake the LORD to serve other gods! [17]It was the LORD our God himself who brought us and our fathers up out of Egypt, from that land of slavery, and performed those great signs before our eyes. He protected us on our entire journey and among all the nations through which we traveled. [18]And the LORD drove out before us all the nations, including the Amorites, who lived in the land. We too will serve the LORD, because he is our God."
>
> [19]Joshua said to the people, "You are not able to serve the LORD. He is a holy God; he is a jealous God. He will not forgive your rebellion and your sins. [20]If you forsake

---

[10] Examples of covenant renewal include *1Kgs 8:1–9:9*, the dedication of the temple; *1 Chronicles 15*, the return of the Ark of the Covenant; *2Chr 34:15–35:19*, reforms by Josiah; *2Chr 29:1–31:21*, reforms by Hezekiah; *Neh 12:26–13:31*, the return from Babylonian exile.

the LORD and serve foreign gods, he will turn and bring disaster on you and make an end of you, after he has been good to you."

²¹But the people said to Joshua, "No! We will serve the LORD."

²²Then Joshua said, "You are witnesses against your-selves that you have chosen to serve the LORD."

"Yes, we are witnesses," they replied.

²³"Now then," said Joshua, "throw away the foreign gods that are among you and yield your hearts to the LORD, the God of Israel."

*²⁴And the people said to Joshua, "We will serve the LORD our God and obey him." (**Josh 24:14-24**)*

This offer of choice is unusual in an OT worship setting. Evidently, some of the children of Israel had been guilty of worshiping deities other than Yahweh. The reference to for-eign gods was not incidental. Followers of pagan gods did not have to choose—they had the option of following mul-tiple gods. Joshua leaves no room for indecision or half-hearted response.

Note that not only is this an act of obedience, but also a recital of God's work, which is uniquely suited to a particular occasion, and an affirmation of the one and | **Joshua leaves no room for indecision or halfhearted response.**

only Creator God. This recitation brings the Israelites to the only possible conclusion: to serve and worship Yahweh only.

COVENANT KEEPING— SACRIFICE

Critical to the keeping of the covenant for ancient Israel was the offering of sacrifices, which was also common in other religions. The sacrificial system relied upon the mediation of priests, appointed by God to act on the behalf of His children. Coming before the holy Yahweh was impossible without His divine intervention. These cultic acts provided form, or ritual, that allowed the created to interact with the Creator.

As we have seen in *Exodus 24* sacrifices accompanied the

cutting of a covenant (see also *Gen 8:20–9:17; 15:1-21; 26:24,25; 35:6-15*). There were other purposes for sacrifices as well. Fellowship, or peace, offerings for example, were made voluntarily as an expression of thankfulness for God's intervention, as the result of a vow, or as appreciation for an unexpected blessing. Fellowship offerings included a communal meal, eaten before God (*Leviticus 3*).

Sacrifices made for atonement of sin were also a part of Israel's regular worship. Sin offerings and guilt offerings required that the blood of an unblemished animal be sprinkled on the altar (*Lev 4:1–5:13; 5:14–6:7*). The sin offering was for "unintentional" sins, which could be sins without conscious intent, sins of ignorance, or sins done intentionally but without defiance. The guilt offering was for offenses that caused loss to the holy things of God or to a neighbor.

The Day of Atonement,[11] when the blood of an animal symbolically atoned for Israel's sin, holds perhaps the greatest significance in our understanding of the corporate gatherings of Israel. This extraordinary day was the only time each year that the High Priest entered into the Holy of Holies. Drawing near to God was made available through the blood that covered the sins of the people. It was only through this ceremony that the sinful could come into the presence of the holy.

It is legitimate to stop here and observe that the sacrifice of Jesus Christ rendered the sacrificial system unnecessary. It does not follow, however, that sacrifices and covenant are irrelevant to worship today. There is value in assessing the nature of sacrifices and reevaluating them in light of our relationship to the Lordship of Christ.

Sacrifices were responses to the person of Yahweh, both who He is and what He had done. They were costly gifts, given back to the Creator, and were about the action itself more than the meaning of the action (see **Brueggemann,**

---

[11] *Lev 16:1-34; 23*. The Day of Atonement is one of the feast days mentioned in ch. 2.

Ancient, 11-24). God had very specific demands for sacrificial rites, but His focus was on the heart of the giver. Nadab and Abi-

> # Sacrifices were responses to the person of Yahweh — who He is and what He had done.

hu, sons of Aaron, offered *"unauthorized fire"* before the Lord and were struck dead (***Lev 10:1-2***). Scripture does not explain what made this offering an abomination to God, but that is inconsequential. The men acted against the Lord's command and paid the price for doing so. When Saul ignored God's commands by sparing the best of the livestock at the defeat of the Amalekites (***1Sa 1:15***), he tried to justify his disobedience by claiming that his actions were meant to please God through sacrifice. Samuel's straightforward response should give us pause today when we place our own interests above God's design:

> *[22]Does the Lord delight in burnt offerings and sacrifices as much as in obeying the voice of the Lord? To obey is better than sacrifice, and to heed is better than the fat of rams. [23]For rebellion is like the sin of divination, and arrogance like the evil of idolatry.* (***1Sa 15:22-23a***)

Only burnt offerings were consumed entirely. Remaining portions of sin and guilt offerings, as well as a token portion of grain offerings were eaten by the priest; the remainder of the peace offerings was shared with the participants. Community is highlighted by sacrificial rituals. The communion is not just with each other, but also with Yahweh. Recall that in ***Exodus 24:11***, Moses, Aaron, Nadab, Abihu, and the seventy elders were allowed to eat and drink in God's presence, and to *"see the God of Israel."*[12] This particular meal stands apart as an example of supernatural table fellowship until God's Son walked this earth and dined with saints and sinners alike.

---

[12]This makes Nadab and Abihu's later act of disobedience all the more striking. To have been in God's actual presence and still act according to one's own wishes is baffling, yet underscores the sinful nature of man and the need for a Savior.

THE NEW COVENANT

As noted, it did not take long for the children of Israel to disobey God's stipulations. Again and again, the covenant was broken and renewed. The only solution for this consistent rebellion was a new kind of covenant, one that was irrevocable. The prophet Jeremiah records God's promise to fulfill this need:

> [31]"The time is coming," declares the LORD,
>   "when I will make a new covenant
> with the house of Israel
>   and with the house of Judah.
> [32]It will not be like the covenant
>   I made with their forefathers
> when I took them by the hand
>   to lead them out of Egypt,
> because they broke my covenant,
>   though I was a husband to them"
>   declares the LORD.
> [33]"This is the covenant I will make with the house of Israel
>   after that time," declares the LORD.
> "I will put my law in their minds
>   and write it on their hearts.
> I will be their God,
>   and they will be my people.
> [34]No longer will a man teach his neighbor,
>   or a man his brother, saying, 'Know the LORD,'
> because they will all know me,
>   from the least of them to the greatest,"
>   declares the LORD.
> "For I will forgive their wickedness
>   and will remember their sins no more." (*Jer 31:31-34*)

The prophets describe the New Covenant as taking the form of a person.[13] Jesus fulfills both sides of the covenant, and all of its conditions. Janice Leonard succinctly summarizes:

> . . . Jesus himself takes on all the elements of the covenant in order to keep it for those who are "in him." He is Servant (*Phil. 2:7*), Lord (*Phil. 2:11*), and Shepherd (*Heb. 13:20-21*). He is the witness to the covenant (*Rev. 1:4-5*). He is the covenant sanctions, the blessing (*Eph.*

[13] See *Isa 42:1-3,6-7; 52:13-14; 53:1-6* for example.

1:3) and the curse (*Gal. 3:13*). He is the Word made flesh (*John 1:1,14*), the text of the new covenant in a language able to be understood, now deposited in the temple of God (*1 Cor. 3:16; Eph. 2:19-22*). He is the sacrifice (*1 Cor. 5:7*) and the covenant meal (*John 6:48-54*), which enact the covenant. He is the garment put on in token of the covenant (*Gal. 3:27*). He is the sign (*Luke 2:34*), our peace (*Eph. 2:14*), and our righteousness (*1 Cor. 1:30*). He has formed his people (*Eph. 2:10*) and named them in order to establish ownership (*Eph. 3:15*). In grateful recognition of God's covenant blessing in the person of Jesus Christ, the church as his royal priesthood is commanded to demonstrate loyalty to the covenant through worship that brings glory to the Lord (*1 Pet. 2:9-10*). (**"Concept,"** 64)

The letter to the Hebrews presents a contrast between old and new. Christ replaces the high priest, the tabernacle, and the covenant. The writer continually makes the case that the new is better than the old. Consider this comparison:

> *[11]When Christ came as high priest of the good things that are already here, he went through the greater and more perfect tabernacle that is not man-made, that is to say, not a part of this creation. [12]He did not enter by means of the blood of goats and calves; but he entered the Most Holy Place once for all by his own blood, having obtained eternal redemption. [13]The blood of goats and bulls and the ashes of a heifer sprinkled on those who are ceremonially unclean sanctify them so that they are outwardly clean. [14]How much more, then, will the blood of Christ, who through the eternal Spirit offered himself unblemished to God, cleanse our consciences from acts that lead to death, so that we may serve the living God!*
>
> *[15]For this reason Christ is the mediator of a new covenant, that those who are called may receive the promised eternal inheritance—now that He has died as a ransom to set them free from the sins committed under the first covenant.* (*Heb 9:11-15*)

The writer of this passage points out the necessity of bloodshed for redemption to be possible. The reference to the ashes of a heifer recalls a method of cleansing one who had been defiled by touching a dead body. A person who failed to be cleansed could not enter the tabernacle and worship. The blood of Christ is better than the blood of animals because it has made us *inwardly* clean, not just *outwardly* clean. What is the outcome of this cleansing? Reminiscent of *"Let my people go, so that they may worship me in the desert,"* the Hebrews passage plainly states that Jesus' unspeakable gift of redemption was offered *"so that we may serve the living God!"*[14]

Not only does being washed by the blood of Christ purify us, so do the waters of baptism:

> Let us draw near to God with a sincere heart in full assurance of faith, having our hearts sprinkled to cleanse us from a guilty conscience and having our bodies washed with pure water. (**Heb 10:22**)

The new covenant was initiated by Jesus Christ at the Last Supper. There the words of the mediator Moses, *"This is the blood of the covenant that the LORD has made with you in accordance with all these words"* (**Ex 24:8**), are reissued by the new mediator, whose once-and-for-all sacrifice would render the old covenant invalid. His words, *"This is my blood of the covenant, which is poured out for many"* (**Mk 14:24**),[15] rang in the ears of the Jewish followers of Jesus, since the words and deeds of Moses and the exodus story were firmly planted in their hearts and minds.

CONCLUSION

Today we should be careful to avoid regular participation in the Eucharistic celebration without revisiting and renewing our covenantal relationship with our Savior. When the gospel story is front and center in our gatherings, covenant cannot be ignored. The promise of God, which has not and will never be broken, is the pulse of the story. Understanding

[14] The word translated "serve" in **Heb 9:14** is the Greek *latreuo*; in other passages it is used to designate priestly service (**Heb 8:5; 9:9**).
[15] Paul includes the word "new" in his account of the meal: *"This cup is the new covenant in my blood"* (**1Cor 11:25**).

the role of covenant in the OT helps us to better grasp the new covenant, as the writer of Hebrews clarifies. The fact that the once-and-for-all sacrifice of Jesus is often forgotten in our daily living highlights our sin and our inability to keep our part of the covenant, which is precisely why it should be remembered in elements inherited from the earliest covenant ceremonies—the Word, the Table, and the cleansing water of baptism.

> **The promise of God, which has not and will never be broken, is the pulse of the story.**

What Do You Say?

1. How might an understanding of *covenant* change the way people view Sunday gatherings? How might it change the way they view their personal worship?

2. Are Word and Table given equal time in your gatherings? Should they be?

3. How are obedience and sacrifice understood today? Are they emphasized as part of every believer's life and duty? Do they appear in our worship rituals?

4. Describe your interaction with symbols, both in worship and in everyday life. Is this interaction different at church than other places? Is it different from your parents or children? What symbols might need to be brought back into our church buildings? Do symbols have a place in *personal* worship?

Simple Plan

a

It was a simple plan. We would ride on our tour bus to the border of Turkey, and because neither our bus nor our guide was allowed to cross over into Greece, we would walk, with our luggage, through the gate a few hundred feet away. A simple plan indeed. But, for some reason, on that bright Sunday morning in January 2005, the Turkish border patrol woke up in a very bad mood.

I will never forget the image of our guide, who had endeared himself to us over the week, walking toward us with his head down and his hands in his pockets, to tell us that, even though he had done this hundreds of times before, we were not going to be allowed to cross in this way on this day. I must stress that we had been treated well all week long and our experience with the Turkish people had been delightful. But there we stood, 37 beleaguered Americans, stuck at the border.

I could not lead out in a song that would compel the guards to let us across. We had with us a veterinarian, who, with all of his knowledge could pull nothing from his bag to change their minds. I am sure that our seminary professor could have preached a fine sermon, but it would have done little as it fell on non-English speaking ears. And even our resident psychology teacher, with his understanding of human nature, could not communicate. We were at the mercy of one mediator—our guide, who spoke both languages and understood the customs of both countries.

Now it turns out that a few hundred American dollars will purchase a ride on another bus from a nearby town. This expense was incurred by our tour company; we were not hungry or thirsty, too cold or too hot. Our lives were not in danger and we were with friends. All that we lost that day was a little time and a little dignity. Later that week, when we returned to Chicago, I was elated to see the sign that said, "U.S. Citizens."

When we approach the Throne of God, our citizenship has been bought for us. No deed that is done, no song that is sung, no sermon that is taught, no gift that is brought gains us entrance there. Rather, we enter by the grace of our Lord Jesus Christ, our only mediator, who understands what it is like to be both human and divine and paid much too high a price for our access there, where He triumphantly and victoriously sits at the right hand of the Father and bids us enter a place we have no right to be.

God's simple plan.

A strange way to save the world.

CHAPTER FOUR

GOD, THE INCARNATE

The Word became flesh and made his dwelling among us.
We have seen his glory, the glory of the One and Only,
who came from the Father, full of grace and truth.

John 1:14

O that birth forever blessed,
when the Virgin, full of grace,
By the Holy Ghost conceiving,
bare the Savior of our race;
And the Babe, the world's Redeemer,
First revealed His sacred face, evermore and evermore![1]

J ust as the encounter with the Creator, Yahweh, at Mt. Sinai in *Exodus 24* provided a turning point in the worship of the nation of Israel, a different kind of divine encounter changed the worship experiences of the created forever. When God became man, He fulfilled the covenant in its entirety. The presence of God, once hidden, now lived among us.

GOD'S REVEALED PRESENCE

The privilege of walking and talk-

---

[1] Aurelius Prudentius (AD 348–413), *Of the Father's Love Begotten.*

ing with the Creator was undoubtedly available to His created before the Fall, because after ignoring His command they found it necessary to hide from Him (*Gen 3:8*). When man sinned, he was "forever renouncing the right and power to fellowship with a holy God" (**Harrison, 9**). But from the moment that man became separated from Him, God began to move His creation back toward fellowship with Him.

The OT recounts many instances of God's presence revealed to man. Enoch, Abraham, Jacob, and Joseph all encountered the presence of the Living God (See *Gen 5:23-25; 17:9-22; 18:1-33; 32:22-32; 39:20-23*). Scripture records that Moses spoke with God *"face to face"* (*Ex 3:11*). God's instruction to Moses

> **From the moment of separation, God began to move His creation back toward fellowship.**

to lead the Israelites out of Egypt marks a new development in the manifestation of God's presence, a people chosen and redeemed. Leading them with a pillar of cloud by day and a pillar of fire by night, "His presence in their midst unifies them, leads them and guides them" (**Harrison, 12**).

In this era of Israel's history, as we have seen, God established a dwelling place for His presence, the tabernacle. J. Carl Laney maintains that the command to build Him a sanctuary "made possible God's promise to restore Himself to His people" (**9**). When the Shekinah[2] glory filled the house (*Ex 40:34,35*), Israel recognized that God was "an active presence and participant in the life of the community" (**Gorman, 20**).

The temple replaced the tabernacle as God's dwelling place, providing a more stationary place for God to dwell. A pattern begins to develop whereby each stage of God's presence becomes more permanent than the last (see **Rogers, 15**).

---

[2] *Shekinah* is a Hebrew word from the root 'to dwell' that is translated as the 'Presence' of God.

Of course, the experiences of the Israelites in the tabernacle and temple only foreshadowed the day when God would become incarnate and "tabernacle" among His people. *John 1:14* declares, *"The Word became flesh and made His dwelling place among us. We have seen His glory, the glory of the One and Only who came from the Father, full of grace and truth."*

Incarnation, from the Latin, *incarnatio*, refers to God becoming man. In Christian thought it is specifically used to describe the Word (Greek, *logos*) being fleshed out in the person of Jesus Christ, as noted by John (*Jn 1:14*). While not found in Scripture, the term "incarnation" has been a part of Christian literature since the fourth century (see **Blackman, 691**).

Harrison beautifully captures the incarnation: "All the meaning and intent of the tabernacle as the meeting-place of God and man find their fulfillment in the

> **While not found in Scripture, the term "incarnation" has been a part of our literature since the fourth century**

person and presence of His Son. Never out of most intimate communion with His Father, nay, the Father was 'abiding' in Him; yet always in close fellowship with man. He was the true temple; in Him God dwelt among men" (**13**). It is the impact of Jesus' life and work upon worship that forms the basis of this chapter.

JESUS' CONCERN FOR WORSHIP

WORSHIP RECEIVED BY JESUS

When God came to dwell on earth, it was in an inauspicious manner, but the arrival was not without praise and thanksgiving. In Luke's Gospel particularly, worship surrounds the events of Christ's birth. Take, for example, Mary's song in *Luke 1:46-55*:

> ⁴⁶And Mary said:
> "My soul glorifies the Lord
> ⁴⁷and my spirit rejoices in God my Savior,

48for he has been mindful
of the humble state of his servant.
From now on all generations will call me blessed,
49for the Mighty One has done great things for me—
holy is his name.
50His mercy extends to those who fear him,
from generation to generation.
51He has performed mighty deeds with his arm;
he has scattered those who are proud in their
inmost thoughts.
52He has brought down rulers from their thrones
but has lifted up the humble.
53He has filled the hungry with good things
but has sent the rich away empty.
54He has helped his servant Israel,
remembering to be merciful
55to Abraham and his descendants forever,
even as he said to our fathers."

Known as the *Magnificat*, this hymn consists of quotations and allusions from the OT. It is closely connected to Hannah's song in **1 Samuel 2:1-10**.[3] Both exalt the name of the Lord, and recite His deeds and merciful intervention. There is a strong similarity with the OT passages we have previously examined as recitations of worship. From the moment He was conceived, interaction with the Son of God resulted in praise, rejoicing, and thanksgiving, with the connection to His Father always emphasized.

> **From the start, interaction with the Son of God resulted in praise, rejoicing, and thanksgiving.**

Upon visiting the newborn child, the shepherds, amazed at what they had seen and heard, *"returned, glorifying and praising God."* Anna, the prophetess, who *"worshiped[4] night and day,"* gave thanks to God when Jesus was presented in the temple. Note that these worshipful outbursts were a result of

---

[3] For other hymns surrounding Christ's birth see also the *Benedictus* of Zacharias, **Lk 1:68-79**; the *Gloria in Excelsis*, **Lk 2:14**, and the *Nunc Dimittis* of Simeon, **Lk 2:29-32**.

[4] *Latreuo*, sometimes translated "served."

a face-to-face encounter with God incarnate. Even though the temple still stood in Jerusalem, the presence of God on earth was enlarging the focus of worship for His people.

Luke gives us insight into those personally impacted by Jesus' birth, but it is Matthew who first uses the word *proskuneo* in the NT (*Mt 2:2,8,11*). The Gentile Magi gave homage to the child that they had come many miles to visit. Nowhere does Scripture suggest that their worship was motivated by any expectation of what this child had done or would do. It seems that being in the presence of the King was enough to cause these kings to bow down and offer gifts in humility and gratitude.

As Jesus touched the hearts and minds of people in His path, worship was often the result. Take, for example, the leper who appeals to Jesus in *Matthew 8:2*. *"A man with leprosy came and knelt [5] before him and said, 'Lord, if you are willing, you can make me clean.'"*

The recognition of Jesus' Lordship also resulted in worship. Even the man possessed by demons fell down before Him in *Mark 5:6*. The disciples worshiped when they saw their Lord walk on water and calm the waves (*Mt 14:33*).

Proskuneo was the result when the disciples saw Jesus following His resurrection (*Mt 28:9*). Matthew makes the disclaimer that, even in the presence of the resurrected Christ, *"some doubted"* (*Mt 28:17*). Indeed, these postresurrection encounters illustrate how difficult it is to define the word "worship." John reports that the disciples were *"overjoyed,"* and that Thomas could only exclaim, *"My Lord, and my God!"*

In all of these examples, Jesus willingly accepted worship. His mission on earth did not discount His pedigree. When the sinful woman had the audacity to waste precious ointment by anointing His feet, He did not rebuke *her*, but those who questioned her act of worship (*Lk 7:36-50*).

---

[5] The word here is *proskuneo*, translated elsewhere as "worshiped." Similar gestures accompany the requests of the ruler in *Mt 9:18* and the Canaanite woman in *Mt 15:25*, on behalf of their daughters, resulting in a resurrection and a healing; each time the word is *proskuneo*.

Yet, even as He received worship from others, He himself offered an example as a worshiper. He was found frequently in the temple and synagogues, teaching and attending festivals, and Luke tells us that He also often withdrew to a solitary place to pray (*Lk 5:16*). He taught His disciples to pray, *"Hallowed be your name,"* (*Mt 6:9; Lk 11:2*) approaching the throne of the Father with reverence and praise.[6]

> **Even as He received worship from others, He was an example of a worshiper.**

In *Luke 10:21*, Jesus expresses joy and praise to God,[7] openly acknowledging that His Father was worthy of such acclamation. He also gave thanks to God with frequency, especially for meals,[8] including the Last Supper.

Jesus' reactions to the temptations He faced in the desert (*Mt 4:1-11; Mk 1:12-13; Lk 4:1-13*) both instruct and exemplify. The tenor of the conversation concerns choice, in essence, *"whom will you worship?"* Jesus answers with quotations from the OT, giving both honor and importance to God's Word.[9] In response to Satan's request to *"bow down and worship me"* (*proskuneo*), He uses both prominent NT words for worship: *proskuneo* (*worship the Lord your God*) and *latreuo* (*serve him only*).[10] Outward physical and verbal expressions of worship are not enough; outward signs through service and wholehearted living speak to the depth of worship as seen through the eyes of Jesus, and throughout both the Old and New Testaments. By denying Himself and serving only His Father, Jesus also shows us that sometimes worship is about what is *not* done.

---

[6] The word translated "hallowed," *hagiazo*, is elsewhere rendered as "sanctified" where it refers to work done *for* people *by* God. Only here does it refer to the holiness of God Himself.

[7] *Agalliao* and *exomologeo*. Luke states that Jesus' joy is *"through the Holy Spirit."*

[8] *Jn 6:11,23; Mk 14:22-23*. The word in these examples is *eucharisteo*, from which the word "Eucharist" is derived.

[9] It is noteworthy that Satan also quoted Scripture, although inaccurately (see *Ps 91:11-12*).

[10] The quotation, from *Deu 6:13*, uses the Hebrew *yare'* (fear) and *'abad* (serve).

JESUS' TEACHINGS ABOUT WORSHIP

On occasion, Jesus' teachings touched on worship. For instance, when offering a gift to God, His followers were to check their attitudes, reconciling with a brother before the offering was made (*Mt 5:23-24*). He harshly condemned the Pharisees as hypocrites for honoring God with their lips but not their hearts. That kind of worship, He said, is in vain, or fruitless.[11] Here Jesus is taking worship out of the context of a particular time and place, instead suggesting that it involves everyday life. The condemnation is against relegating worship to rules and regulations. This passage is often ignored in our discussions of worship, perhaps because it hits too close to home. If we were to place both our corporate and private worship under scrutiny, we might on occasion hear this indictment echoing in our ears.

> **Jesus takes worship away from a particular time and place to involve it in everyday life.**

All of these encounters and teachings give insight into worship as understood and practiced by the incarnate God. But His unexpected conversation with an ordinary and seemingly unimportant woman provides us with the most comprehensive teaching concerning *proskuneo* in the NT.

Jesus and the Samaritan Woman

A significant difference between worship in the Old and New Testaments is a change in the understanding of the temple. This cataclysmic shift becomes evident in the encounter between Jesus and the Samaritan woman in the *fourth chapter of John*.

> [1]The Pharisees heard that Jesus was gaining and baptizing more disciples than John, [2]although in fact it was

---

[11]The word for worship here is *sebomai*, which means "to revere," and is used ten times in the New Testament. Jesus is quoting from *Isa 29:13*, where the word is again from the Hebrew "fear."

not Jesus who baptized, but his disciples. ³When the Lord learned of this, he left Judea and went back once more to Galilee.

⁴Now he had to go through Samaria. ⁵So he came to a town in Samaria called Sychar, near the plot of ground Jacob had given to his son Joseph. ⁶Jacob's well was there, and Jesus, tired as he was from the journey, sat down by the well. It was about the sixth hour.

⁷When a Samaritan woman came to draw water, Jesus said to her, "Will you give me a drink?" ⁸(His disciples had gone into the town to buy food.)

⁹The Samaritan woman said to him, "You are a Jew and I am a Samaritan woman. How can you ask me for a drink?" (For Jews do not associate with Samaritans.)

¹⁰Jesus answered her, "If you knew the gift of God and who it is that asks you for a drink, you would have asked him and he would have given you living water."

¹¹"Sir," the woman said, "you have nothing to draw with and the well is deep. Where can you get this living water? ¹²Are you greater than our father Jacob, who gave us the well and drank from it himself, as did also his sons and his flocks and herds?"

¹³Jesus answered, "Everyone who drinks this water will be thirsty again, ¹⁴but whoever drinks the water I give him will never thirst. Indeed, the water I give him will become in him a spring of water welling up to eternal life."

¹⁵The woman said to him, "Sir, give me this water so that I won't get thirsty and have to keep coming here to draw water."

¹⁶He told her, "Go, call your husband and come back."

¹⁷"I have no husband," she replied.

Jesus said to her, "You are right when you say you have no husband. ¹⁸The fact is, you have had five husbands, and the man you now have is not your husband. What you have just said is quite true."

¹⁹"Sir," the woman said, "I can see that you are a prophet. ²⁰Our fathers worshiped on this mountain, but you Jews claim that the place where we must worship is in Jerusalem."

²¹Jesus declared, "Believe me, woman, a time is coming when you will worship the Father neither on this mountain nor in Jerusalem. ²²You Samaritans worship what you do not know; we worship what we do know, for salvation is from the Jews. ²³Yet a time is coming and has now come when the true worshipers will worship the Father in spirit and truth, for they are the kind of worshipers the Father seeks. ²⁴God is spirit, and his worshipers must worship in spirit and in truth."

²⁵The woman said, "I know that Messiah" (called Christ) "is coming. When he comes, he will explain everything to us."

²⁶Then Jesus declared, "I who speak to you am he."

Much is often made concerning the incongruities of this encounter. In the time of Jesus, Jews considered Samaritans to be half-breeds and avoided them at all cost. The Samaritan religion was based only on the Pentateuch, and worship was conducted on Mount Gerizim, where their temple had once stood. Therefore, Gerald Borchert points out, "the climate of relations between the two was scarcely conducive to good communication or self-giving acceptance" (**200**). Similarly, Jewish men did not talk to women in public. The time of day implies that she was avoiding other women who would have come in the early morning to draw water. Yet, here was Jesus, speaking to a Samaritan woman who apparently had questionable morality. As shocking as this dismissal of social and religious conventions must have been to her, what He told her about worship had to have been equally as surprising.[12]

In answer to her question, *"Our fathers worshiped on this mountain, but you Jews claim that the place where we must worship is in Jerusalem,"* Jesus boldly proclaims that *"a time is coming when you will worship the Father neither on this mountain nor in Jerusalem"* (***Jn 4:20-21***). Previous to His conversation with the Samaritan woman, Jesus had both cleansed the temple of corruption and abuse and declared that if it were destroyed He could raise it in three days (***Jn 2:13-25***)! Now Jesus dismisses the earthly temple, followed by a rare decla-

---

[12] It is interesting to contrast this conversation with the one carried on between Jesus and Nicodemus in **John 3**. Two totally different people were taught about water and Spirit, and living by truth. See **Walvoord, 284**. It seems that this woman gained a better grasp of Jesus' teaching and exhibited greater faith than did Nicodemus, a Jewish leader.

ration of His Messiahship (*"I who speak to you am He," **v. 26***), the implication being that He has come to replace the temple. Later, the stoning of Stephen (**Acts 7**) would be due in large part to his insistence that *"the Most High does not live in houses made by men"* (**v. 48**).

Jesus' answer to the woman's simple question appears to be equally simple:

> Yet a time is coming and has now come when the true worshipers will worship the Father in spirit and truth, for they are the kind of worshipers the Father seeks. God is spirit, and His worshipers must worship in spirit and in truth. (**Jn 4:23-24**)

Borchert expresses Jesus' concern for worship, stating that "he turned the conversation away from place of worship to nature of worship" (**207**). Jesus does not stress specifics concerning the content of worship. If He had laid down rules similar to those the Jews had learned under the Old Covenant, churches today would have a much easier job in planning Sunday worship. But as He, the very fulfillment of

Jesus initiated a call for worship more concerned with the heart than the form.

the New Covenant, stood before the Samaritan woman, He initiated a call for worship that is more concerned with the heart of the worshiper than the form that it takes.

Spirit and Truth

While this is the most complete passage about *proskuneo* in the NT, Jesus' assertion that true worshipers will worship God in spirit and truth leaves us with a bit of ambiguity. We will, however, attempt to comprehend the nuances of these two words in order to make application for today.

Most scholars agree that the word "spirit," translated from the Greek word, *pneuma*, refers to the human spirit. However, the word, coupled with the acknowledgement that "God is spirit," connects the human to the divine. Considering Jesus' previous discussion concerning "living water," which Donald Guthrie denotes is "a well known symbol of the Holy Spirit" (**528**), it is probable that Jesus is alluding to a time in the near future when the Holy Spirit will direct the human spirit (see *Jn 7:37-39*). Richard Averbeck deduces that "the direct correspondence and functional connection between the divine Spirit and the human spirit is of the utmost importance in worship" (**102**). The Holy Spirit's work in worship is discussed in chapter 6, where we will discover yet another transition of God's presence, from Christ dwelling "with" us to Christ dwelling "in" us.

In John's writings the Greek word *aletheia* translated as "truth" often means "authenticity," "divine reality," or "revelation" (**Bultmann, 39**). Jesus calls Himself the "true bread," for example, *"he who comes down from heaven and gives life to the world"* (*Jn 6:33*). Unlike the manna supplied during the exodus that sustained only the physical, Jesus is the sustainer, and source, of all of life. He is also the *"true light"* (*Jn 1:9*), and the *"true vine"* (*Jn 15:1*). In *John 1*, the Word made flesh is *"full of truth"* (*v. 14*) and claims that He *is* the truth (*Jn 14:6*).

Bultmann understands worship in truth to mean "not just in pure knowledge but as determined by God's own reality, in *pneuma*, and by the revelation made in Jesus (**39**). A.C. Thiselton agrees that *aletheia* conveys the idea of reality, contrasting it with "whatever the situation may look like on the surface" (**890-891**). Consequently he reasons, "Those who worship God in Spirit and in truth are not those who worship in sincerity and inwardness. The Samaritans are not criticized for lacking sincerity. True worship is that which accords with reality, which men grasp on the basis of revelation" (**891**). C.H. Dodd's definition of *en aletheia* is "on the plane of reality," meaning that truth "comes through Jesus" (**175**).

It is impossible in this context to separate spirit and truth into two separate entities. Recognizing this close connection, Mark Scott inter-

> **It is impossible to separate spirit and truth into two separate entities.**

prets this text as a call to authenticity, suggesting that "Jesus might be emphasizing qualities in the worshiper and not the realms in which the worship takes place." "Maybe," he says, "Jesus is saying, 'Come before me in genuineness of heart.'" Echoing Dodd's assertion that truth "comes through Jesus," he concludes that the key to becoming authentic is "nothing less than salvation by Christ and discipleship in Him, where we are delivered from the cancer of self!" (**"Worship"**).

Often this passage is used to justify the need for both emotions and knowledge in worship. The critical issue, however, is the necessity of recognizing the Messiah's role in worship. It seems unlikely that John, with his consistent usage of *aletheia* to refer to Jesus, would be using the word here to simply refer to human knowledge. Without the gospel, worship in spirit and truth is not possible. Jesus boldly proclaims the dissolution of the earthly temple and later will leave the Holy Spirit to inhabit the worship of believers.

In today's world, spirituality is being sought through many different avenues, not just the church. When lost persons visit our gatherings, they are often looking for authenticity, for something real, solid, and true. Placing Jesus Christ at the center of these occasions and relying on the Holy Spirit to work through and in us meets both the needs of people and the design of our Father for worship: spirit and truth.

Through the incarnation, God's presence transitioned from "with" to "in." Jesus promised "another Counselor to be with you forever—the Spirit of truth" (*Jn 14:16-17*). Paul exhorts, *"Don't you know that you yourselves are God's temple?"* (*1Cor 3:16*). "In Acts and the Epistles the believer is set forth, historically and doctrinally, as indwelt by the very presence of God" (**Rogers, 15**). When Jesus ascends to His Father, the gatherings of those early groups of believers are still infused with His presence, yet newly empowered by the Holy Spirit. It is therefore helpful to examine the practices of the church in her infancy.

NEW TESTAMENT GATHERINGS

The Synagogue

H.H. Rowley claims it was the synagogue that "set the pattern for Christian and Muslim worship, as well as the worship which survived the destruction of the temple [AD 70] for Judaism" (213). Derived from a term that referred to any type of gathering, the exact origins of the Jewish synagogue are debated; many believe that it developed out of necessity during the Babylonian exile. Whatever the case, worship in the synagogue took on a very different form than that of the temple. Having no priestly rituals, synagogue worship emphasized praise, prayer, and instruction. Frank Senn reports that the reading, exposition, and application of Scripture were at the heart of synagogue worship (70-71). O.S. Rankin credits the synagogue service with giving the Christian service its pattern of praise-prayer-reading of Scripture-homily or sermon (175).[13] John Frame notes that while God gave specific instructions concerning the sacrificial worship of the temple, He left the arranging of the synagogue services up to the people (23). Jesus taught in the synagogue (*Lk 4:15-16*) and regularly attended services there, which suggests that it was a valuable place for worship and teaching.

Acts 2:46 records that the early believers *"continued to meet together in the temple courts."* According to Hill, "The early church continued to worship, pray, preach, and teach in the temple until the persecution of Christians in Jerusalem associated with the stoning of Stephen" (185). Underhill credits the temple rituals for "those primitive symbols and references which abound in the New Testament and still continue to play an essential part in its liturgies and hymns"

> **Sacrifice and offering were not forgotten, but viewed through new eyes.**

---

[13] Rankin observes that this pattern is used in the part of the service that is called pro-anaphoral, i.e., the part prior to the Eucharist.

(213). The themes of sacrifice and offering were not forgotten, but viewed through the eyes of those who claimed a new redemption.

THE "BIG FOUR" — ACTS 2

Acts 2 provides insight into the worship practices of the early church by illustrating its daily activities: *"They devoted themselves to the apostles' teaching and to the fellowship, to the breaking of bread and to prayer"* (*Acts 2:42*)."[14] Because of the Holy Spirit-inspired power of these practices, they have remained at the center of Christian worship for two millennia. We will therefore delve into each one a bit more closely.

The Apostles' Doctrine

There is no example that gives us a glimpse of the content of the messages given to believers in the NT church. Neither does the book of Acts give a clear description of what comprised *"the apostles' teaching"* (*didache*). Ajith Fernando believes that it likely included "explanations of the nature of salvation, the person and work of Christ, the commands of Christ and other features of the Christian life, and the message of the kingdom" (120). The apostles are described as teachers of the good news (*Acts 5:42*); Paul and Barnabas are noted as both teaching (*didasko*) and preaching (*euangelizo*) (*Acts 15:35*). The latter word has a more specific relationship to the "good news," or the gospel. While attending synagogue services in Antioch (*Acts 13*), Paul is asked to give a word of exhortation (*paraklesis*) to an audience of both Jews and Gentiles. He does so by providing a narrative of God's saving acts in the history of Israel and culminating in the resurrection, which he proclaims as "good news"(*euangelizo*)![15]

---

[14] Literally, "the prayers" (Greek *hai proseuchai* – plural).

[15] Apparently the Gentiles did a good job of spreading the word as Scripture reports that the following week the *whole city* gathered to hear the word. This is the pattern in the NT: the gathered community scatters and continues to spread the gospel.

It is notable that Paul's letters were meant to be read in the assembly. For example, *"After this letter has been read to you, see that it is also read in the church of the Laodiceans and that you in turn read the letter from Laodicea"* (**Col 4:16**); *"I charge you before the Lord to have this letter read to all the brothers"* (**1 Th 5:27**). Besides these admonitions, he uses language that suggests this intent. Ralph Martin says:

> It seems clear that Paul had before his mind's eye, as he wrote his Letters or dictated them, a picture of the Church assembled for public worship. The introductory greetings and opening prayers of thanksgiving are couched in no commonplace language but reflect, by their fullness of expression and unusual vocabulary, the liturgical life of the Churches. (*Early*, 33)

Because of this connection between the Epistles and the gathered church, it seems likely that the teaching associated with the early church was primarily concerned with the encouragement, exhortation, and edification of the Body.

> **The teaching of the early church was concerned with encouragement, exhortation, and edification of the Body.**

The sermons that *are* recorded in Acts are evangelistic, but are found outside the assembly, most notably Peter at Pentecost (**Acts 2:14-41**) and Paul in Athens (**Acts 17:22-31**). A common word in the NT is *kerusso*, which, simply put, means to proclaim the gospel. It is used of Jesus, as well as Paul, Philip, Peter, and other heralds of the good news. Another term, *kerygma*, is only found eight times, none in Acts. It is also closely associated with the gospel story, but refers to the message itself more than the act of proclaiming it.

Certainly the custom of biblical instruction has remained consistent throughout the history of the church and remains a strong component today. It is the *type* of instruction that is sometimes debated. Are we to take **Acts 2:42** at face value, and insist upon teaching only in our gatherings?[16] Or are we to

---

[16] Alexander Campbell held to the opinion that the use of *didache* in this passage meant just that (**Hieronymus**, 4-5). C.H. Dodd expounds on this idea in *The Apostolic Preaching and Its Developments*.

The gospel is never irrelevant, whether taught or preached.

allow the Sunday gathering to assume the role of the evangelist and preach for the purpose of winning converts? If one looks at the content of teaching (as suggested by the Epistles) and preaching (as recorded in the NT), the redemption story—the life, death and resurrection of Jesus Christ—is at the center. Paul proclaims it to believers and nonbelievers alike, even at the risk of stirring up a considerable amount of trouble, as it did in Athens. It is the pulse of the proclamation at Pentecost and at the heart of the conversion of the Ethiopian Eunuch. The Epistles are teeming with it, and Revelation resounds with it. The gospel is never irrelevant, whether taught or preached.

The Fellowship

The Greek word translated "fellowship" is *koinonia*, denoting "participation," especially with a close bond. (**Hauck, 798**). Richard Foster defines it as "deep inward fellowship in the power of the Spirit" (**143**). It generally means "a group of people bound together in 'communion' or 'fellowship' by what they have in common with each other." The **Book of Acts** makes it clear that this "communion" included sharing possessions with those in need, praising God together, and being devoted to one another. Paul sees this relationship as essential to followers of Jesus Christ: *"Share [koinoneo] with God's people who are in need. Practice hospitality"* (**Rom 12:13**). The writer of Hebrews links it with the "sacrifice of praise": *"And do not forget to do good and to share [koinonia] with others, for with such sacrifices God is pleased"* (**Heb 13:16**).

It is interesting to note that most churches devoted to the restoration of NT Christianity cling to the apostles' doctrine, the breaking of bread, and the prayers in framing contemporary gatherings. The more elusive concept of fellowship, however, has often been relegated to potluck dinners and home Bible studies. While these types of gatherings do go a long way toward building a true community, perhaps bodies of believers could further explore methods of promoting *koinonia* within the context of the Sunday morning assembly.

> **Perhaps bodies of believers could further explore ways to promote *koinonia* within the regular assembly.**

Koinonia is a privilege of Christian life unparalleled by any other affiliation. This unique quality is highly relevant in today's society, where community is desirable. Those who are unable to find it in their broken world may gravitate toward a body where it is boldly displayed.

The Breaking of Bread

F.F. Bruce states that "the 'breaking of bread' probably denotes more than the regular taking of food together: the regular observance of what came to be called the Lords' Supper seems to be in view." (79). Oscar Cullman reasons that the designation "breaking of bread," an unusual expression to designate a meal, "indicates that those present were conscious of performing at the same time an act of special significance" (318-319). Other references indicate that the early Christians met for both a regular meal and the Lord's Supper (*Acts 2:46*), and that they met purposefully to break bread on the first day of the week (*Acts 20:7*).[17]

The Prayers

Prayer was of utmost importance to the NT church; it was the first activity they were found engaged in following the Ascension: *"They all joined together constantly in prayer, along with the women and Mary the mother of Jesus, and with his brothers"* (*Acts 1:14*). The Apostles found it necessary to appoint helpers to minister to the flock, in order that they themselves

Chapter 4
God the Incarnate

---

[17] The Lord's Supper is also related to redemption, covenant, and the Holy Spirit's work in worship and is discussed in chapters 2, 3, and 6 respectively, as well as the discussion on 1 Corinthians which follows.

Prayer was the first activity the disciples were found engaged in following the Ascension. might be devoted to prayer and the word (*Acts 6:1-6*). These servants were then prayed over as they were set apart for the work of the Lord. Paul and Silas prayed in jail (*Acts 16:25*) as part of their unconventional worship service, and the church at Antioch prayed for Paul and Barnabas (*Acts 13:2-3*).

As noted, Jewish practices continued to permeate the worship of the early church, and praying was no exception. Therefore the prayers (*proseuche*) mentioned in *Acts 2:42* almost certainly have some affinity with the prayers the new Christians had learned as Jews. Ken Read theorizes that the term may "refer to the 19 prayers that were recited by rote every day in the synagogue" (**95**).[18] Bruce concurs with this possibility, but believes that Luke is primarily referring to "their own appointed seasons for united prayer" (**80**). Whatever the case, prayer was undoubtedly an essential element of the assembly from the very beginning of the church. Geoffrey Bromiley summarizes, "A genuine Christian service without [prayer] is almost unthinkable" (**107**). Not only does the service itself rely upon the gracious intervention of God, but praying in the assembly instructs the flock in the art of prayer, as Jesus taught His disciples (*Mt 6:9-13*).

PAUL'S CONCERN FOR WORSHIP— 1 CORINTHIANS

While the Acts passage paints a picture of the early church gathered, *1 Corinthians* is instructive in nature. The city of Corinth was a thriving city and home to many pagan deities. While the church there was gifted by the Holy Spirit, it was apparently also affected by its pagan surroundings and

[18] The *Sh'moneh Esrei* ("eighteen"), also known as the *Amidah* ("standing"), are a set of ancient Jewish prayers. A nineteenth prayer was added later. These prayers are still used today by the Jewish community.

influenced by secular social status. Therefore, Paul's letter is directed toward a church that is having some very specific problems which had resulted in divisions and

The church of Corinth was apparently affected by its pagan surroundings and secular social status.

quarrels. As these issues are addressed, we gain insight into the apostle's concerns for worship in the assembly.

THE ELEMENTS OF NEW TESTAMENT GATHERINGS

Although Paul in no way suggests a particular structure for worship gatherings in his letter, he does list some of the elements of early Christian worship—a hymn, a word of instruction, a revelation, a tongue or an interpretation (*1Cor 14:26*). The letter also offers glimpses into elements that might have been present in NT gatherings: responsive Amens (*1Cor 14:16*), holy kisses (*1Cor 16:20*), prostration (*1Cor 14:25*), and healing (*1Cor 12:9*) to name a few. Prayers are offered spontaneously, through the work of the Holy Spirit (*1Cor 14:14*); recalling, however, that Paul borrowed liturgical language for his letters, expecting them to be read in the assembly, it is likely that the prayers, doxologies, and benedictions offered in this letter and others were a regular part of early Christian gatherings. He does not dwell on the necessity of one component over another, but rather is concerned with the spirit in which they are offered, expecting each one to participate using the gifts God has given him. He insists that all is done *"for the strengthening of the church,"* admonishing the believers to show deference to one another, speaking in tongues only if an interpreter is present so that all may praise God together. *"If you are praising God with your spirit, how can one who finds himself among those who do not understand say 'Amen' to your thanksgiving, since he does not know what you are saying? You may be giving thanks well enough, but the other man is not edified"* (*1Cor 14:16-17*).

THE LORD'S SUPPER

The efficacy and nature of the Lord's Supper was important to Paul, and he spends most of *1 Corinthians 11* dealing with its appropriate celebration. In the first century, the Lord's Supper would have been part of an *agape* meal (or love feast), a common meal where members brought food to contribute. Evidently the body in Corinth was abusing the meal because the rich were eating first so that the poor had nothing. This greediness was causing division among members. Ben Witherington indicates that "the division is between the haves and have-nots, such that some are going hungry at the meal while others are gorging themselves and getting drunk" (**53**). Gordon Fee points out that the issue for Paul is not "with the drunkenness of one but with the hunger of the other" (**"History,"** 28). The poor are being ignored, and therefore the meal cannot celebrate the unity that has been made possible by the work of Jesus Christ.

As Paul deals with these difficulties, we gain a better understanding of his opinions concerning this important element of worship. He does not suggest a particular manner in which the elements must be distributed or handled, but rather a particular manner in which they should be understood. Steering the Corinthians away from their selfishness, he turns their attention back

> **Paul does not suggest how the elements must be distributed or handled, but how they should be understood.**

to the institution of the Supper by the Lord Jesus Christ. This places emphasis on the salvation story and allows for reenactment as part of every Sunday celebration.

William Baird views the Lord's Supper as multifaceted:

> It is God's saving action, continually reenacted in the life of His people. Its traces of Passover observance remind the faithful that God has led them out of Egypt. Its stress upon the Lord's death makes real God's supreme redemptive act in the midst of history for all

men. Its continual repetition provides men of ongoing history with the opportunity to confess the crucified Christ. Its pointing to the future grants hope to the world, joy to the faithful, trust in the victory of God. Indeed, participation in the Supper of the Lord illuminates the whole history of salvation. (133-134)

Paul's words in *1 Corinthians 11:27-29* require examination, as they are often repeated at the Table, sometimes to the exclusion of the rest of the chapter. He admonishes,

> *Therefore, whoever eats the bread or drinks the cup of the Lord in an unworthy manner will be guilty of sinning against the body and blood of the Lord. A man ought to examine himself before he eats of the bread and drinks of the cup. For anyone who eats and drinks without recognizing the body of the Lord eats and drinks judgment on himself.*

Taking this text out of context may result in a Communion observance that is lopsided and self-centered. The context suggests that Paul is concerned with the *"unworthy manner"* of which the Corinthians were guilty, that is the divisiveness and lack of concern for one another. While *"to examine himself"* does suggest an inward focus, the warning directly follows Paul's exhortation to *"proclaim the Lord's death until he comes"* (*v. 26*). Therefore, *"recognizing the body of the Lord"* appears to refer back to Paul's recalling of the body and blood of Jesus, necessitating an examination of the believer's relationship to Jesus and requiring more than a recital of daily trespasses.

Additionally, *The New Interpreter's Bible* reminds us that

> in Paul's thought the body of Christ can never be separated from the members who by God's grace are incorporated into it. So 'discerning the body' is Paul's shorthand way of talking about an individual's assessment of two distinguishable but inseparable matters: how well one's life relates to Christ and how well one's love ties one to others who, though many, are one body in Christ. (Sampley, 936)

The body of Christ can never be separated from the members in it.

Alexander Campbell speaks eloquently on this matter:

> Upon the loaf and upon the cup of the Lord, in letters which speak not to the eye, but to the heart of every disciple, is inscribed, "*When this you see, remember me.*" Indeed, the Lord says to each disciple, when he receives the symbols into his hand, "This is my body broken for *you*. This is my blood shed for *you*." The loaf thus constituted a representation of His body—first whole, then wounded for our sins. The cup is thus instituted a representation of His blood—once His life, but now poured out to cleanse us from our sins. To every disciple he says, "For *you* my body was wounded; for *you* my life was taken." In receiving it the disciple says, "Lord, I believe it. My life sprung from thy suffering; my joy from thy sorrows; and my hope of glory everlasting from thy humiliation and abasement even to death." Each disciple, in handing the symbols to his fellow disciple, says, in effect, "You, my brother, once an alien, are now a citizen of heaven; once a stranger, are now brought home to the family of God. You have owned my Lord as your Lord, my people as your people. Under Jesus the Messiah we are one. Mutually embraced in the Everlasting arms, I embrace you in mine; thy sorrows shall be my sorrows, and thy joys my joys. Joint debtors to the favor of God and the love of Jesus, we shall jointly suffer with Him, that we may jointly reign with Him. Let us, then, renew our strength, remember our King, and hold fast our boasted hope unshaken to the end." (**Christian System**, 273).

LESSONS FROM 1 CORINTHIANS

There are some serious implications here for churches today. First, the heart of the worshiper needs to be consistently cultivated, rather than focusing entirely upon methods or particular elements used in corporate worship. Second, leaders should attempt to become aware of the giftedness of each member of the body, that it might be used for the glory of God. This may include musical talent, artistry, hospitality, teaching, and a plethora of other God-given abilities. Finally, the edification of the whole is more important than the pleasure of one.

Noting that there might be unbelievers in the assembly, Paul does not imply that the gathering should cater to them. Rather, he suggests that when believers worship wholeheartedly, unbelievers will fall down[19] and worship God, exclaiming, *"God is really among you!"* (*1Cor 14:25*). Paul concludes his exhortation about the assembly by reminding his readers that *"everything should be done in a fitting and orderly way"* (*1Cor 14:40*), accenting the corporate nature of the assembly. Individuals were not to focus on their personal preferences, but on that which would build up the body of Christ.

> **The edification of the whole is more important than the pleasure of one.**

The impact of OT worship upon the early church is unmistakable. Music, for example, continued to be prevalent in the gathered community. Paul commands its usefulness to the church at Colossae: *"Let the word of Christ dwell in you richly as you teach and admonish one another with all wisdom, and as you sing psalms, hymns and spiritual songs with gratitude in your hearts to God"* (*Col 3:16*). The exact nature of these three types of musical entities is uncertain. Psalms (*psalmos*) almost certainly refers to the Psalms of David, which, even to this day, remain as the pulse of Christian song. Hymns (*hymnos*) carry the simple meaning of a sacred song, and spiritual songs (*pneumatikos ode*) imply a relationship to the Holy Spirit. Hymns may have been adapted from Jewish songs for a new community and are possibly reflected in the hymns discussed in chapter 2; spiritual songs, it has been suggested, may have been more spontaneous and improvised in nature. Whatever the nuances of these three terms, Paul was not stuttering. He must have had a reason for including three different types of song here and in his Ephesian letter (*Eph 5:19*). The real issue was not the *style* of

---

[19] This is Paul's only usage of the word, *proskuneo*, and it is used in connection with unbelievers! Note, however, that their reaction is to the *presence of God*, as manifested in the work of the Holy Spirit.

> **The real issue was not the style of the song but the heart condition of the singer and the unity of the body.**

the song but the *heart condition* of the singer (*let the word of Christ dwell in you richly*) and the *unity* of the body (*as you teach and admonish one another*).

By now it should be clear that the study of NT worship relies upon the OT. God, the Creator and Redeemer, gave specific instructions concerning worship to His people, the Israelites. Covenant making, the sacrificial system, the tabernacle and temple, the establishment of liturgical practices, and emphasis on holy living all point to Jesus.

JESUS CHRIST AT THE CENTER—REVELATION

When God became man, He became the focus of worship on earth; in His Revelation to John we see that He is also the focus in heaven.

> [22]*I did not see a temple in the city, because the Lord God Almighty and the Lamb are its temple. The city does not need the sun or the moon to shine on it, for the glory of God gives it light, and the Lamb is its lamp.* [23]*The nations will walk by its light, and the kings of the earth will bring their splendor into it.* (**Rev 21:22-23**)

> [11]*I saw heaven standing open and there before me was a white horse, whose rider is called Faithful and True. With justice he judges and makes war.* [12]*His eyes are like blazing fire, and on his head are many crowns. He has a name written on him that no one knows but he himself.* [13]*He is dressed in a robe dipped in blood, and his name is the Word of God.* [14]*The armies of heaven were following him, riding on white horses and dressed in fine linen, white and clean.* [15]*Out of his mouth comes a sharp sword with which to strike down the nations. "He will rule them with an iron scepter." He treads the winepress of the fury of the wrath of God Almighty.* [16]*On his robe and on his thigh he has this name written:* KING OF KINGS AND LORD OF LORDS. (**Rev 19:11-16**)

The temple has been ultimately and irreversibly replaced, and light has overcome forever. Jesus is True, as seen in *John 4*, and the Word, as seen in *John 1*. He is Faithful and Just, characteristics of Yahweh well documented by the Psalmist. He is Sovereign above all, ruling now and for eternity. He thus shares worship with His Father.

CONCLUSION

It was noted in chapter 1 that *proskuneo* is used only in the Gospels and Revelation, with one exception (see *1Cor 14:25*). The true presence of God inspires, in fact, *requires*, worship. In the Gospels, He walked this earth; in Revelation He reigns and is worshiped unceasingly. In Acts, His Church, empowered by the Holy Spirit, shifts her worship from the rituals of sacrifices to the joys of newness in Christ. The requirements for authentic worship, according to Jesus, are spirit and truth.

What Do You Say?

1. If you could ask Jesus one question about worship, what would it be? Based on His response to the Samaritan woman, how do you think He would answer?

2. Of the "Big Four" in *Acts 2*, which is most important in your context? Why do you think this is true? What is the least important? What could you do to emphasize it more?

3. What other elements found in NT gatherings are prevalent today? Lacking?

4. The NT provides a description of a gathered community. Should this be considered a prescription for worship gatherings today? Why or why not?

5. Do you believe that Jesus is at the center of most Sunday gatherings? Why or why not?

6. If the apostle Paul wrote a letter to the church today concerning worship practices, what do you think he might say?

Forgiveness

A few years ago, when my nephew was not quite four years old, he tore up a book that he had checked out of the library. I cannot tell you the extent of the damage, but the infraction was great enough that he was required by his parents to return it and apologize.

His mother took him to the library, and the kind and gentle librarian asked, "Grant, is there something you need to tell me?" Unable to get out a response, he simply shook his head no. She went off to do some librarian things, then returned and asked again, "Grant, do you want to tell me something?" Again, he only shook his head. This went on for quite some time, until finally he was able to blurt out, "I'm sorry I tore up your book!" My sister-in-law paid the fine and they went home.

I can't be certain what was going on in his little mind, but I have a hunch.

I don't think he knew . . .

. . . that he was already forgiven.

CHAPTER FIVE

GOD, THE SAVIOR

And we have seen and testify
that the Father has sent his Son
to be the Savior of the world.
1 John 4:14

Long lay the world in sin and error pining
'Til He appeared, and the soul felt its worth.
A thrill of hope, the weary world rejoices,
For yonder breaks a new and glorious morn. . . .[1]

WAITING FOR A SAVIOR

Near the end of the HBO mini-series, *Band of Brothers*, a group of soldiers from Easy Company find themselves at an abandoned concentration camp where hundreds of inmates are still imprisoned. Starving and near death, the prisoners begin to emerge from the barracks, uncertain as to their fate. When they realize that they are about to be freed, they embrace the stunned Americans with gratitude. One emaciated man even kisses the cheek of his liberator. It is a difficult scene to watch, but it identifies a

I. Waiting for a Savior
   A. Savior in the Old Testament
   B. Savior in the New Testament
II. Corporate Confession
   A. Public Declarations of Allegiance
   B. Confession of Sin
     1. Psalm 51
     2. Isaiah 6
     3. New Testament Confession
III. Forgiveness—Dispelling the Darkness
IV. Salvation Belongs to God and to the Lamb
V. Conclusion

---

[1] *O Holy Night*, words by Placide Cappeau de Roquemaure, 1847, trans. by John S. Dwight.

human emotion that most of us cannot begin to imagine: what it is like to wait a very long time for a savior.

The nation of Israel, however, understood waiting. At the time of Christ's coming, the world, as the prophet Isaiah convincingly preached, was wrapped in the darkness of sin and was in need of light that only a Savior could bring: *"So justice is far from us, and right-eousness does not reach us. We look for light, but all is darkness; for brightness, but we walk in deep shadows"* (**Isa 59:9**).[2]

> ## The world was wrapped in the darkness of sin and in need of light that only a Savior could bring

Today many Christians have difficulty identifying with this darkness, in part because our corporate worship often ignores its existence. Although we sing, pray to, and exult in the God who saves, we do not want to look squarely in the face of sin. Yet recognizing God as Savior requires that we are able to recognize what we have been saved *from*.

SAVIOR IN THE OLD TESTAMENT

The OT understanding of "savior" was primarily that of being delivered from death, disease, or harm.[3] It was applied to earthly leaders, such as the judges, but was most often reserved for Yahweh, who had delivered Israel from the bondage of slavery. *Psalm 18* lays out the OT theme of salvation beautifully:

> [1]*I love you, O LORD, my strength.*
> [2]*The LORD is my rock, my fortress and my deliverer;*
>   *my God is my rock, in whom I take refuge.*
>   *He is my shield and the horn of my salvation, my*
>   *stronghold.*
> [3]*I call to the LORD, who is worthy of praise,*
>   *and I am saved from my enemies. (vv. 1-3)*
> [30]*As for God, His way is perfect;*

---

[2] Darkness versus light is one of Isaiah's favorite metaphors. See also **Isa 5:20,30; 8:22; 9:2; 29:15,18; 42:7,16; 45:7; 49:9; 50:10; 58:10; 60:2; 61:1**.
[3] *Yasha'*, meaning "to be saved, delivered, or liberated." See **2Sa 22:3; 1Chr 16:35; Psalm 18; Isa 17:10; Mic 7:7**.

> the word of the Lord is flawless.
> He is a shield
>   for all who take refuge in him.
> ³¹For who is God besides the Lord?
>   And who is the Rock except our God?
> ³²It is God who arms me with strength
>   and makes my way perfect. (*vv. 30-32*)
> ⁴⁶The LORD lives! Praise be to my Rock!
>   Exalted be God my Savior!
> ⁴⁷He is the God who avenges me,
>   who subdues nations under me,
>   ⁴⁸who saves me from my enemies.
> You exalted me above my foes;
>   from violent men you rescued me.
> ⁴⁹Therefore I will praise you among the nations, O LORD;
>   I will sing praises to your name.
> ⁵⁰He gives his king great victories;
>   he shows unfailing kindness to his anointed,
>   to David and his descendants forever. (*vv. 46-50*).

Note the worship words that surround the recognition of God as Savior. The psalmist responds with love, praise, exaltation, and singing. Thanksgiving and praise are once again seen as responses, this time to the God of salvation. The subtitle informs us that David *"sang to the Lord the words of this song when the LORD delivered him from the hand of all his enemies and from the hand of Saul."*

Now experiencing a time of peace, David looks back on episodes of hopelessness and desperation, recognizing the constant presence and intervention of God's mighty hand.

> **Thanksgiving and praise are once again seen as responses, this time to the God of salvation.**

The descriptors for God in this passage are numerous and vivid. He is seen as a rock, fortress, deliverer, shield, and horn of salvation.⁴ All of these titles signify that He has saved the psalmist from despair, even death, and that He will continue to do so. Furthermore, the whole nation of Israel is

---

⁴ "Horn" was a metaphor for strength or power.

under God's watchful eye and in His providential care. He is a strong and mighty Savior.

Charles Spurgeon implores, "He who rescues us from deserved ruin should be very dear to us. In heaven they sing, 'unto Him that loved us and washed us in His blood,' the like music should be common in the assemblies of the saints below" (280). From darkness comes light, which should be consistently before us as we worship together in the assembly.

SAVIOR IN THE NEW TESTAMENT

In the NT, God is referred to as Savior eight times.[5] The first NT usage is found in the midst of Mary's song of worship: *"My soul glorifies the Lord and my spirit rejoices in God my Savior, for he has been mindful of the humble state of his servant"* (*Lk 1:47*). Although this marvel of doxological faith seems to be personal in nature, Mary is looking forward to a salvation that is for all people. Zechariah picks up the theme in his prophecy:

> [68]*"Praise be to the Lord, the God of Israel,*
>   *because he has come and has redeemed his people.*
> [69]*He has raised up a horn of salvation for us*
>   *in the house of his servant David*
> [70]*(as he said through his holy prophets of long ago),*
> [71]*salvation from our enemies*
>   *and from the hand of all who hate us—*
> [76]*And you, my child, will be called a prophet of the*
>   *Most High;*
>   *for you will go on before the Lord to prepare the*
>   *way for him,*
> [77]*to give his people the knowledge of salvation*
>   *through the forgiveness of their sins.* (*Lk 1:68-71,76-77*)

Both hymns are reminiscent of David's exaltation of God the Savior in *Psalm 18*, using the same kind of language to describe Him. They serve as a turning point between the deliverer of the OT and His specific work of salvation through Jesus Christ.

---

[5] *Soter*, meaning "Savior, Deliverer, or Preserver." See *Lk 1:47; 1Tm 1:1; 2:3; 4:10; Tts 1:3; 2:10; 3:4; Jude 25*.

The sixteen other uses of "savior" in the NT are connected to Jesus, a name derived from the Hebrew word for "the Lord saves." When the angel of the Lord informs Joseph that the child to be borne by Mary will be called by this name, a new expectation of promise is set forth for Israel, *"He shall save his people from their sins"* (*Mt 1:21*).

This word for "savior" is found twice in the Gospels, once at the birth of Jesus (*Lk 2:11*),[6] and the second following the Samaritan woman's evangelistic crusade (*Jn 4:42*), as well as in Acts and the Epistles (*Acts 5:31; 13:23; Eph 5:23; Php 3:20; 2Tm 1:10; Tts 2:13; 3:6; 2Pet 1:1; 1:11; 2:20; 3:2; 3:18; 1Jn 4:14*). In these passages the focus is clearly on deliverance or salvation from sin. Besides references to Christ as Savior, the noun, "salvation," and verb form "to save," are used frequently in the NT, also in reference to being rescued from the consequences of sin.

CORPORATE CONFESSION

Responding to God as Savior through praise and thanksgiving is more potent if we are cognizant of sin and the darkness from which we have been lifted. There is another response, however, that has been long removed from many Christian churches, the corporate response of repentance and confession. Dismissed because of its "liturgical" roots, or perhaps simply because it seems to us to be too somber for our generally upbeat gatherings, confession must be revived.

> **Praising God as Savior is more potent if we recognize the sin and darkness from which we have been lifted.**

It must always be remembered, however, that because of the saving work of Jesus Christ those who belong to Him are able to approach it with the assumption that they are already forgiven.

---

[6] The first time in the New Testament the word "savior" is used specifically of Jesus.

Public Declarations of Allegiance

Confession in Scripture is generally understood in one of two ways: as confession of faith, or as confession of sin. "On the one hand, confession[7] means to declare publicly a personal relationship with and allegiance to God. It is an act of open joyful commitment made to God in the presence of the world, by which a congregation or individuals bind themselves in loyalty to God or Jesus Christ" (Torrance, 219). These types of confessions, especially in the OT, are accompanied by thanksgiving, praise, and sacrifice. We have already identified the importance of creedal declarations in corporate worship, which give voice to this kind of confession.

In the NT, creedal statements have the distinctive of proclaiming, or confessing, Jesus as Lord (*Php 2:11*). When called before the Sanhedrin for healing a crippled man, as well as preaching the resurrection, Peter claimed that salvation was available only through Jesus:

When called before the Sanhedrin, Peter claimed that salvation was available only through Jesus.

[8]*Rulers and elders of the people!* [9]*If we are being called to account today for an act of kindness shown to a cripple and are asked how he was healed,* [10]*then know this, you and all the people of Israel: It is by the name of Jesus Christ of Nazareth, whom you crucified but whom God raised from the dead, that this man stands before you healed.* [11]*He is*

"'the stone you builders rejected,
which has become the capstone.

[12]*Salvation is found in no one else, for there is no other name under heaven given to men by which we must be saved.* (Acts 4:8b-12)

Peter and John were then commanded *"not to speak or teach in the name of Jesus"* (**Acts 4:18**), an instruction they ig-

---

[7] *Homologeo*, meaning to say the same thing as another, i.e., to agree with, assent, or to admit or declare one's self guilty of what one is accused of.

nored, resulting in continued growth of the infant church. The proclamation of the gospel story is consistent throughout the early Christian centuries, a practice that often resulted in persecution because to proclaim Jesus was to deny an earthly ruler or pagan god.

> **The proclamation of the gospel story is consistent throughout the early Christian centuries.**

Verbal confessions not only served as a witness; Paul connects them specifically with salvation:

> *⁹That if you confess with your mouth, "Jesus is Lord," and believe in your heart that God raised him from the dead, you will be saved. ¹⁰For it is with your heart that you believe and are justified, and it is with your mouth that you confess and are saved. (**Rom 10:9-10**)*

We may deduce that creedal statements of belief—the life, death, and resurrection of Jesus, His work that bought our salvation—still have benefit for us today. Both believers and non-believers need to hear the story proclaimed over and over.

CONFESSION OF SIN

It is the confession of sin to which we now give attention. John declares,

> *⁸If we claim to be without sin, we deceive ourselves and the truth is not in us. ⁹If we confess our sins, he is faithful and just and will forgive us our sins and purify us from all unrighteousness. ¹⁰If we claim we have not sinned, we make him out to be a liar and his word has no place in our lives. (**1Jn 1:8-10**)*

The use of "confess" here refers to the acknowledgement of "sin and guilt in the light of God's revelation, and is thus generally an outward sign of repentance and faith" (**Torrance, 219**).

John writes from the assumption that it is tempting to ignore sin altogether, a practice which is dishonest and harmful. Stephen Smalley explains, "The claim to be sinless is a self-deception. For sin is a fact of life, and characteristic of those who are Christians, as well as those who are not. . . .

We *ought* to acknowledge our sin; and if we do God responds" (**30-31**). In the NT, the promise of forgiveness is never far behind an honest admission of sin. This should also hold true for our corporate gatherings where the gospel is the center of our worship.

Confession of sin for early Christians would have been understood in the context of Jewish law. According to George Bowman, ". . . the confession in Old Testament days was quite clear in its implications of sorrow for sin and the intention to amend life. A change in one's life was expected." The rituals surrounding sin offerings and guilt offerings, for example, both require confession and restitution:

> ⁵When anyone is guilty in any of these ways, he must confess in what way he has sinned ⁶and, as a penalty for the sin he has committed, he must bring to the LORD a female lamb or goat from the flock as a sin offering; and the priest shall make atonement for him for his sin. (**Lev 5:5-6**)

> ⁵The LORD said to Moses, ⁶"Say to the Israelites: 'When a man or woman wrongs another in any way and so is unfaithful to the LORD, that person is guilty ⁷and must confess the sin he has committed. He must make full restitution for his wrong, add one fifth to it and give it all to the person he has wronged. ⁸But if that person has no close relative to whom restitution can be made for the wrong, the restitution belongs to the LORD and must be given to the priest, along with the ram with which atonement is made for him. (**Num 5:5-8**)

Psalm 51

Perhaps the best way to understand confession is to view it through the lens of one in need of forgiveness. *Psalm 51* provides a vivid example of the pain and anguish that we all face when confronted with our sin.

> ¹Have mercy on me, O God
>   according to your unfailing love;
> according to your great compassion
>   blot out my transgressions.
> ²Wash away all my iniquity
>   and cleanse me from my sin.

³For I know my trans-
     gressions,
   and my sin is always
     before me.
⁴Against you, you only, have
     I sinned
   and done what is evil in
     your sight,
so that you are proved right when you speak
   and justified when you judge.
⁵Surely I was sinful at birth,
   sinful from the time my mother conceived me.
⁶Surely you desire truth in the inner parts;
   you teach me wisdom in the inmost place.

⁷Cleanse me with hyssop, and I will be clean;
   wash me, and I will be whiter than snow.
⁸Let me hear joy and gladness;
   let the bones you have crushed rejoice.
⁹Hide your face from my sins
   and blot out all my iniquity.

¹⁰Create in me a pure heart, O God,
   and renew a steadfast spirit within me.
¹¹Do not cast me from your presence
   or take your Holy Spirit from me.
¹²Restore to me the joy of your salvation
   and grant me a willing spirit, to sustain me.
¹³Then I will teach transgressors your ways,
   and sinners will turn back to you.
¹⁴Save me from bloodguilt, O God,
   the God who saves me,
   and my tongue will sing of your righteousness.
¹⁵O Lord, open my lips,
   and my mouth will declare your praise.
¹⁶You do not delight in sacrifice, or I would bring it;
   you do not take pleasure in burnt offerings.
¹⁷The sacrifices of God are a broken spirit;
   a broken and contrite heart,
   O God, you will not despise.
¹⁸In your good pleasure make Zion prosper;
   build up the walls of Jerusalem.
¹⁹Then there will be righteous sacrifices,
   whole burnt offerings to delight you;
   then bulls will be offered on your altar. (Ps 51:1-19)

> # Psalm 51 provides a vivid example of the anguish we all face when confronted with our sin.

Classified as one of the seven "penitential" Psalms,[8] this response to David's sin with Bathsheba is well known and often recited. The recognition that the man after God's own heart acknowledged and confronted his personal sin both comforts and instructs us. We identify with what Thomas Chalmers describes as "the effusion of a soul smarting under the sense of a recent and great transgression" (457).

Although it is the result of one man's cry for mercy, the designation, "to the chief musician," implies that the poem was intended for public service. Therefore *Psalm 51* is equally adaptable to a gathered community, offering a kind of template for a prayer of confession. David begins by appealing to God's mercy, a frequent occurrence in the lament Psalms.[9] Knowing that he has no right to God's forgiveness, he nevertheless stands before the throne on the basis of God's unfailing love and compassion.

> **Knowing he has no right to forgiveness, he stands before the throne on the basis of God's love.**

David continues with an impassioned recognition of his sin. He is willing to lay open his heart, acknowledging that which has made it unclean. According to Franz Delitzsch, this is an act of true penitence, "not a dead knowledge of a sin committed, but a living sensitive consciousness of it, to which it is ever present as a matter and ground of unrest and pain" (135).

Following his admission of guilt, David offers a prayer for restoration and forgiveness. He seeks cleansing, renewed joy, and a pure heart. Again we see a connection to corporate gatherings, as much of the imagery here, such as cleansing, washing, and blotting out, suggests worship rituals. Priests

---

[8] See also *Pss 6, 32, 38, 102, 103, 143*. "In each of these psalms, the writer acknowledges his sin to Yahweh and asks for forgiveness. Hence the term *Penitential*: these psalms voice the repentant attitude of the speakers and demonstrate God's loving forgiveness when sin is confessed" (Travers, 250).

[9] See, for example, *Pss 4:1; 6:2; 31:9; 41:4,10; 56:1; 86:3*. See ch. 1 for a discussion of the Lament Psalms.

were required to wash before entering God's presence. The unclean were instructed to present themselves before a priest in order to be made pure by being sprinkled with water.[10]

"The real point, however, is that by God's action, the psalmist has been or will be transformed" (**McCann**, *Theological*, **104**). David then offers the appropriate response of thanksgiving and praise for God's intervention and act of deliverance. *Psalm 51* "strikes a balance between David's repentance and God's glory, showing us in its overall effect how important it is in every aspect of our lives for us to know God as He reveals himself in the Bible" (**254**).

Isaiah 6

A study of confession would not be complete without a glimpse at Isaiah's encounter with the Almighty. Seen by many as the most explicit biblical example of a worshiper responding to God, *Isaiah 6:1-5* leaves no doubt that the presence of Yahweh evokes confession:

> [1]*In the year that King Uzziah died, I saw the Lord seated on a throne, high and exalted, and the train of his robe filled the temple.* [2]*Above him were seraphs, each with six wings: With two wings they covered their faces, with two they covered their feet, and with two they were flying.* [3]*And they were calling to one another:*
>
> *"Holy, holy, holy is the LORD Almighty;*
>   *the whole earth is full of his glory."*
>
> [4]*At the sound of their voices the doorposts and thresholds shook and the temple was filled with smoke.* [5]*"Woe to me!" I cried. "I am ruined! For I am a man of unclean lips, and I live among a people of unclean lips, and my eyes have seen the King, the LORD Almighty."*

The first part of this divine encounter reinforces our previous discussion concerning transcendence (see ch. 1). The

---

[10] See **Ex 30:18-21, Num 8:7; Lev 14:1-9; 2Chr 4:6, Eze 36:25, and Heb 10:22**, "Let us draw near to God with a sincere heart in full assurance of faith, having our hearts sprinkled to cleanse us from a guilty conscience and having our bodies washed with pure water." "Washed with pure water" implies making purification from sin, or to make clean in a Levitical sense. John uses this same concept in **1Jn 1:9**.

themes of majesty, holiness, and divine presence illustrated in the tabernacle are exhibited here in the extreme. Walter Brueggemann says, "We are here at the core of holiness from which is decreed all that happens everywhere in creation. The song of the heavenly choir begins in holiness and ends in glory, both terms acknowledging the odd, overwhelming otherness of God" (*Isaiah*, 59).

This magnificent depiction of Yahweh and the subsequent worship makes even more striking Isaiah's complete devastation. He recognizes his own sinfulness after encountering God's holiness and purity. Which of us, in our cozy, contemporary worship settings, have so thoroughly encountered God that we are completely undone by Him?

To attempt to ignore that which makes one uncomfortable dismisses an essential part of worship. Marva Dawn suggests that "as God reveals himself in all God's truth, our response will be like that of Isaiah. 'Woe to me, for I am ruined.' (*Isa 6:5*, NASB—Martin Luther translated it, 'I am annihilated'). The more we encounter the holy God in our worship, the more we will recognize our utter sinfulness and be driven to repentance. This, too, is an essential part of our praise" (*Reaching Out*, 90).

> **Which of us have so thoroughly encountered God that we are undone?**

It would be unconscionable for us to leave Isaiah in a state of ruin and repentance; the next part of his encounter with the Almighty is where we find hope. *"See, this has touched your lips; your guilt is taken away and your sin atoned for"* (*Isa 6:7*). With a hot coal, representing the fire necessary for burnt sacrifices, the prophet is freed from both sin *and* guilt. This is a remarkable gift. Isaiah has done nothing to deserve such treatment. Yet now he is qualified to be in the presence of God, to fulfill the command to *"be holy as I am holy."* The natural and obvious reaction is one of service, *"Here am I. Send me!"*

It is often thought that confession is necessary to enter the presence of God, and this notion has impacted the structure of contemporary worship gatherings. The experience of Isaiah suggests, however, that confession may be a response to the acknowledgement of the transcendent One. Isaiah also reminds us that a worship encounter does not end with praise, confession or forgiveness, but with change of heart and call to action.

> **A worship encounter does not end before a change of heart and call to action.**

New Testament Confession

We now return to the NT, where confession is related to the work of Jesus Christ, accomplished through His life, death, and resurrection. Here there is hope for all who confess Jesus as Lord.

Like John, James exhorts us to confess our sins, taking it one step further to a public declaration:

> *Therefore confess your sins to each other and pray for each other so that you may be healed. The prayer of a righteous man is powerful and effective. (**Jas 5:16**)*

The form of the verb, "confess,"[11] implies a repeated action. Kurt Richardson understands James to mean that "the whole fellowship of believers should be characterized by mutual confessing of sin" (236). There is no indication as to the occasion of these confessions, nor does James suggest that a recital of the actual sins committed is required. The emphasis seems to be on a humble admission to sinning. More importantly, those who hear the confessions are instructed to pray for the confessor, so that he might be able to resist committing the same infraction in the future. This provides a way to *"carry each other's burdens,"* as Paul teaches in *Galatians 6:2*.

In a world ravaged with evil and doubt, many attend church anticipating comfort, which makes some congregations resistant to confession. But Dietrich Bonhoeffer insists that this need for comfort is a byproduct of confronting sin:

---

[11] *Exomologeo*, translated, "to confess," is the most commonly used word for the confession of sin in the New Testament. See also *Mt 3:6, Mk 1:5, Acts 19:18*.

But it is the grace of the Gospel, which is so hard for the pious to understand, that it confronts us with the truth and says: You are a sinner, a great, desperate sinner; now come, as the sinner that you are, to God who loves you. He wants you as you are; He does not want anything from you, a sacrifice, a work: He wants you alone. God has come to save the sinner. Be glad! (**110-111**).

FORGIVENESS— DISPELLING THE DARKNESS

We began this chapter with the Incarnate Word bringing light into a dark world. Forgiveness, or atonement, in the OT was possible only through sacrifices and only through the mediation of a priest. If we place ourselves in the world of the ancients, perhaps we can better grasp the significance of the once-and-for-all sacrifice of Jesus Christ:

> [23]*Now there have been many of those priests, since death prevented them from continuing in office;* [24]*but because Jesus lives forever, he has a permanent priesthood.* [25]*Therefore he is able to save completely those who come to God through him, because he always lives to intercede for them.*
>
> [26]*Such a high priest meets our need—one who is holy, blameless, pure, set apart from sinners, exalted above the heavens.* [27]*Unlike the other high priests, he does not need to offer sacrifices day after day, first for his own sins, and then for the sins of the people. He sacrificed for their sins once for all when he offered himself.* [28]*For the law appoints as high priests men who are weak; but the oath, which came after the law, appointed the Son, who has been made perfect forever.* (**Heb 7:23-28**)

If we are not diligent in reminding ourselves of the weight and debt of sin absent the loving intervention of God, we can become too comfortable in our acceptance of His graceful forgiveness. While the blood of goats and bulls is no longer

We must remind ourselves not to become too comfortable in expecting His graceful forgiveness.

necessary and Jesus has performed for us the ministry of the High Priest, we still have an offering to bring.

> [15]Through Jesus, therefore, let us continually offer to God a sacrifice of praise—the fruit of lips that confess His name. [16]And do not forget to do good and to share with others, for with such sacrifices God is pleased. (**Heb 13:15-16**)

The *"sacrifice of praise"* commanded here has a kinship with the fellowship offerings of the OT, which were voluntary gifts.[12] The offerings carried with them the idea of confessing, or acknowledging, the faithful intervention of God. They were characterized by a communal meal eaten by the worshiper and his family. The Hebrews writer has once again transplanted his audience from the old to the new. Sacrifice is now continuous and is a byproduct of the believer's relationship with Jesus. God is pleased, he says, with doing good and sharing with others. The work of Jesus, that is, salvation for all, produces fruit of praise and service in the believer.

SALVATION BELONGS TO GOD AND TO THE LAMB

To this point we have seen that the worship of God, who is Creator and Redeemer, extends to His Son, the Incarnate. The Book of Revelation explicitly attests to this truth. In Revelation the symbol most commonly associated with Jesus is that of the Lamb[13] who was slain, which links Him to the process of salvation:

> [9]After this I looked and there before me was a great multitude that no one could count, from every nation, tribe, people and language, standing before the throne and in front of the Lamb. They were wearing white robes and were holding palm branches in their hands. [10]And they cried out in a loud voice:

---

[12] See **Leviticus 3; 7** for regulations surrounding the fellowship offering.
[13] In Revelation, Jesus is called *arníon* (lamb), 28 times. The word *amnós* is used in the rest of the NT (**Jn 1:29,36; Acts 8:32; 1Pet 1:19**) to describe Jesus as an innocent lamb who atones for our sins.

> *"Salvation belongs to our God,*
> *who sits on the throne,*
> *and to the Lamb."*
>
> *[11]All the angels were standing around the throne and around the elders and the four living creatures. They fell down on their faces before the throne and worshiped God, [12]saying:*
>
> *"Amen!*
> *Praise and glory*
> *and wisdom and thanks and honor*
> *and power and strength*
> *be to our God for ever and ever.*
> *Amen!"* (**Rev 7:9-12**)

The Book of Revelation is concerned with what is yet to come, the Second Coming of Christ. Robert Lowery notes that "John summarizes the Christian life in terms of salvation as a past fact, a present duty, and a future hope" (**46**). The final battle will result in either salvation or judgment for all:

> *[1]After this I heard what sounded like the roar of a great multitude in heaven shouting:*
>
> *"Hallelujah!*
> *Salvation and glory and power belong to our God,*
> *[2]for true and just are his judgments.*
> *He has condemned the great prostitute*
> *who corrupted the earth by her adulteries.*
> *He has avenged on her the blood of his servants."*
>
> *[3]And again they shouted:*
>
> *"Hallelujah!*
> *The smoke from her goes up for ever and ever."*
>
> *[4]The twenty-four elders and the four living creatures fell down and worshiped God, who was seated on the throne. And they cried:*
>
> *"Amen, Hallelujah!"* (**Rev 19:1-4**)

CONCLUSION

There is never any doubt in Revelation that salvation belongs only to God and to His Son. Because the first-century world often gave the name "savior" to its kings, the power of this title was potent for the times. It should be the same for us, because the world in which we live is too willing to give allegiance to others. This is why the salvation story, the gospel, should never be missed

> **Our Sunday worship is fruitless if it does not involve our hearts, our actions, and the rest of the week!**

on any given Sunday. We accomplish this by proclaiming *with our mouths*, that Jesus is Lord and that we have sinned and are willing to repent and live a life worthy of the gift of salvation. This can be done through recitations, singing, or praying. But it is fruitless if it does not also involve *our hearts, our actions*, and the rest of the week!

What Do You Say?

1. Can you identify with the need for a Savior? Do you think our Sunday gatherings ignore the reality of sin? Name a hymn or song that speaks to our sinfulness.

2. Is there a lack of confession in the church today, both private and corporate? Is there a need for it? How might it be accomplished in your context?

3. What does David, the man after God's own heart, teach us about the need to confess?

4. In what ways do modern Christians offer a "sacrifice of praise"?

Baffled
by
Mystery

One night I am telling my nieces a story about the world's largest toy store, which comes to life at night. One of the rooms in the store contains hundreds of dolls of all kinds. Some are as small as your little finger, while others are as large as your mom. During the magical evening hours the dolls have a fashion show, trying on clothes and shoes and all manner of accessories.

My niece raises her hand. She is six.

"What about the dolls as small as your finger?"

"What about them?"

"How do they fit into the clothes?"

Quick thinking:

"The clothes are magic. They fit whoever tries them on."

"Well, okay then."

She is able to accept toys that come to life at night.

But one-size-fits-all baffles her.

Sometimes I wonder if our belief in the story falls short of accepting mystery.

CHAPTER SIX

GOD, THE MASTER

Therefore, I urge you, brothers,
in view of God's mercy,
to offer your bodies as living sacrifices,
holy and pleasing to God—
this is your spiritual act of worship.
Romans 12:1

Ideally, worship is a Spirit-led symphony of doxology,
giving praise to God, proclaiming what He has done and
is doing, and what the human response should be.
(**Paige, 412**)

WORSHIP IS A LIFE OF SURRENDER

Throughout Scripture, God is depicted as Lord, or Master, over our part of the divine story. He owns all of creation. It is the supreme act of worship to give oneself over to God completely, as a servant who loves his master. All of the responses that have been previously discussed risk becoming inauthentic and false if we are unwilling to live a life of consistent surrender.

SERVICE IN THE OLD TESTAMENT

For the ancient Israelites, servanthood was a known entity in no way divorced from true worship. Notice how in ***Deuteronomy 10:12-21*** the Creator and Redeemer requires both obedience and service:

> [12]And now, O Israel, what does the LORD your God ask of you but to fear the LORD your God, to walk in all his ways, to love him, to serve the LORD your God with all your heart and with all your soul, [13]and to observe the LORD's commands and decrees that I am giving you today for your own good?
>
> [14]To the LORD your God belong the heavens, even the highest heavens, the earth and everything in it. [15]Yet the LORD set his affection on your forefathers and loved them, and he chose you, their descendants, above all the nations, as it is today. [16]Circumcise your hearts, therefore, and do not be stiff-necked any longer. [17]For the LORD your God is God of gods and Lord[1] of lords, the great God, mighty and awesome, who shows no partiality and accepts no bribes. [18]He defends the cause of the fatherless and the widow, and loves the alien, giving him food and clothing. [19]And you are to love those who are aliens, for you yourselves were aliens in Egypt. [20]Fear the LORD your God and serve him. Hold fast to him and take your oaths in his name. [21]He is your praise; he is your God, who performed for you those great and awesome wonders you saw with your own eyes.

Gary Hall notes that the five demands God makes here (fear, walk, love, serve, and observe) are key responses in Deuteronomy. "Each one on its own or in combination expresses the similar thought: God requires wholehearted devotion from his people. . . .what God desires most of all from his people are not sacrifices (that is religious ritual) but justice and loyalty" (**197-198**). Notice that these responses are once again made as a result of the recital of God's acts of salvation.

---

[1] *'Adon,* meaning "firm, strong, lord, master," generally refers to the owner of slaves or servants. See ***Gen 24:39; Ex 21:1-8***, etc. The term refers to God here. See also ***Pss 97:5; 114:7; 136:3; 147:5; Isa 1:24; 31:1; 10:16,33; Mal 3:1***. The term is frequently juxtaposed with *Yâhovah* (indicated in English by all capital letters), which is God's proper name.

The prophet Isaiah reiterates this truth in his scathing indictment of Israel's worship.[2]

> [10]Hear the word of the LORD,
>   you rulers of Sodom;
> listen to the law of our God,
>   you people of Gomorrah!
> [11]"The multitude of your sacrifices—
>   what are they to me?" says the LORD.
> "I have more than enough of burnt offerings,
>   of rams and the fat of fattened animals;
> I have no pleasure
>   in the blood of bulls and lambs and goats.
> [12]When you come to appear before me,
>   who has asked this of you,
>   this trampling of my courts?
> [13]Stop bringing meaningless offerings!
>   Your incense is detestable to me.
> New Moons, Sabbaths and convocations—
>   I cannot bear your evil assemblies.
> [14]Your New Moon festivals and your appointed feasts
>   my soul hates.
> They have become a burden to me;
>   I am weary of bearing them.
> [15]When you spread out your hands in prayer,
>   I will hide my eyes from you;
> even if you offer many prayers,
>   I will not listen. **(Isa 1:10-15a)**

All of the acts of worship that have thus far been acceptable, including sacrifices, incense, festivals, and even prayer, are now rebuffed by God! Why? Brueggemann states, "Yahweh rejects them because Israel's gestures of worship are no longer vehicles for a serious relationship" (*Isaiah*, 17). The offerings are not accompanied by a life of obedience, holiness, and justice, and are therefore dishonest. They have become tiresome to God. Going through the motions of worship is not enough. Acceptance of God as Master manifests itself in complete allegiance, resulting in holy living and acts of service.

---

[2] Isaiah is not the only prophet to take issue with Israel's worship. See *Hos 6:6; Am 5:21-25; Mic 6:6-8; Jer 7:21-23*.

In the NT, "lord"[3] refers to God or Jesus, as well as to humans who possess "servants."[4] Paul was able to use the metaphor of slavery in his letters because it was an accepted part of life for his readers. *Ephesians 6:5-9* demonstrates both the culture of the day and the realignment of "master" from earthly to heavenly.

> *5Slaves [doulos], obey your earthly masters [kurios] with respect and fear, and with sincerity of heart, just as you would obey Christ. 6Obey them not only to win their favor when their eye is on you, but like slaves [doulos] of Christ, doing the will of God from your heart. 7Serve wholeheartedly, as if you were serving the Lord, not men, 8because you know that the Lord will reward everyone for whatever good he does, whether he is slave or free.*
>
> *9And masters, treat your slaves in the same way. Do not threaten them, since you know that he who is both their Master [kurios] and yours is in heaven, and there is no favoritism with him.*

The Greek verb, *douleuo*, or serve, used in this passage was the word most commonly associated with slaves and masters in NT times. Peterson observes that because "it conveyed the notion of total dependence and of obedience without any right of personal choice, it was generally not regarded as an appropriate expression of service to the gods in Greek religion" (**167**). Servants of Christ, however, were expected to give their lives over to God with fervor and dedication. Theirs was not a burdensome service, but one of freedom and joy.

Servants of Christ were expected to give their lives over to God with fervor and dedication.

---

[3] *Kurios*, meaning "he to whom a person or thing belongs, about which he has power of deciding." Most uses of the word are translated "lord." The word, *epistates*, or "master" is used to address Jesus several times (**Lk 5:5; 8:24,45; 9:33,49; 17:3**); *despotes*, also translated "master" is used in **2Pet 2:1** and **Jude 4** and of God in **Lk 2:29; Acts 4:24**; and **Rev 6:10**. These words are basically synonyms; the point is that in the New Testament, Jesus was understood to be the master and His followers were His servants.

[4] *Doulos*, slave, servant, bondman.

Romans 12:1

As noted in chapter one, the verb more often affiliated with worship is *latreuo* also translated "to serve." Its noun form (*latreia*) is found in **Romans 12:1**:

> Therefore, I urge you, brothers, in view of God's mercy, to offer your bodies as living sacrifices, holy and pleasing to God—this is your spiritual act of **worship**.

This passage cannot be understood apart from the sacrificial system. The words "offer," "sacrifices" and "act of worship" would have conjured up images of cultic worship. Paul expects his readers to make this analogy. We have seen in the above OT passages that sacrifices were, in and of themselves, not enough for God. He required obedience and holy living as well. It should come as no surprise that Paul moves from the old sacrificial system to a new one, built on God's mercy supremely seen in the work of Jesus Christ. The offering of

God desires that we relinquish ourselves, our bodies, in full allegiance to Him.

animals and other sacrifices are no longer necessary. Instead God desires that we relinquish ourselves, our bodies, in full allegiance to Him.

A few verses earlier, Paul uses the same noun (*latreia*) to indicate ritual worship:

> Theirs is the adoption as sons; theirs the divine glory, the covenants, the receiving of the law, the temple **worship** and the promises. (**Rom 9:4**)

Jack Cottrell insists that there is no contradiction here. "The point is" he says, "that all Christian living is worship offered up to God. Public, corporate worship is special and must not be neglected, but that is not the only part of the Christian life that may be called 'worship.' Christians must do *everything* 'for the glory of God' (**1Cor 10:31**), and whatever is done for his glory is an act of worship" (**Romans,** 2:312).

The term "spiritual act of worship" is derived from a rendering of the Greek, *logikos latreia*. The word *logikos* is used

Chapter 6 God the Master

157

only twice in the NT[5] and has also been translated "reasonable," "rational," or "appropriate." The important issue is that Paul is referring to worship that differs from the offering of sacrifices, pointing toward the worship of everyday life.

Peterson addresses a possible misunderstanding concerning this phrase:

> If Paul's expression is translated 'spiritual worship,' there is a danger of accenting the inwardness of Christian worship and not taking sufficient account of the fact that we are to yield our bodies to God's service. On the other hand, the translation 'rational worship' may only suggest a contrast between the offering of rational beings and the sacrifice of irrational animals. The mind is certainly central to Paul's perspective here, but the focus is not simply on rationality. (**176**)

The NIV solves this problem by using "spiritual *act* of worship," suggesting, rightly, that worship, or service, is something that requires action on the part of the worshiper. This is true whether in Sunday gatherings or daily life. Paul was not suggesting, however, that one solitary act was, or would ever be, enough but that worship is a continual, ongoing lifestyle.

Service and Ministry

Latreuo, plays a prominent role in Hebrews, a letter which is in large part a contrast between the Old and New Covenants, particularly in relationship to the tabernacle.[6] Because the sacrificial system was at the heart of the Old Covenant, it stands to reason that a new interpretation of worship is necessary. Therefore, *latreuo* loses some of the cultic emphasis and is used to describe the inner worship of the heart. Horst Balz proposes that this sense of *latreuo* "indicates both the connection of Christian worship with the old worship of the

---

[5] A term used by classical philosophers, meaning "belonging to speech" or "belonging to reason." The first sense is not found in the NT. The second sense is found here and *1Pet 2:2*, *"Like newborn babies, crave pure spiritual milk, so that by it you may grow up in your salvation."* See **Kittel, 143**.

[6] *Heb 8:5; 9:9,14; 10:2; 12:28; 13:10*. See also ch. 3.

priests and the discontinuity of the worship, in that the new ministry encompasses the entire life of the believer" (345).

Two other words set side by side highlight the importance of whole-life worship in the NT, *leitourgia*[7] and *diakonia*,[8] which both indicate "service" or "ministry." The English word, "liturgy," a commonly misunderstood word among certain Protestant groups, is derived from *leitourgia*. Its secular usage had to do with laboring at one's own expense for the good of the community. Rodney Clapp explains:

> In Roman society, "to build a bridge for a public road across a stream on one's private property would constitute a liturgy." Military service at one's own expense was an act of liturgy. The wealthy sought favor by sponsoring "liturgies"—huge dramas for the entertainment of the citizenry. *Leitourgoi*, or, roughly, "liturgists," in the secular Greek usage of the times referred to government officials. (80)

The term came to be applied to cultic acts, and is often used to denote the service of priests as they offer prayers or sacrifices. In Scripture it carries with it the connotation of "work," or service, done in a gathering of believers for the purpose of glorifying God. Like *latreuo*, it is found most notably in the book of Hebrews because it often refers to ministering, or serving, both in the old and new tabernacles. Jesus is referred to in this letter as *leitourgikos*, or the one who performs the service of the high priest in the true, heavenly sanctuary (*Heb 8:2*) (**Hess, 552**). His death and resurrection have accomplished, once and for all, the ministry formerly performed by the earthly high priests, entrance into the presence of God:

---

[7] *Lk 1:23; Heb 8:6; 9:21; Php 2:17; 2Cor 9:12*. The verb form, *leitourgeo*, occurs in *Lk 1:23; Rom 15:27*; and *Heb 10:11*. The adjective form, *leitourgikos*, refers to the angels ministering spirits in *Heb 1:14*. A rarer form of the noun, *leitourgos*, is used in *Heb 8:2* in reference to Jesus Christ, and in *Rom 15:16* in reference to Paul; in *Rom 13:6, Php 2:25*, and *Heb 1:7* the references are not cultic in nature.

[8] Along with *diakonos* and the verb form *diakoneo* this word group is used over ninety times in the NT. See for example, *Acts 6:2; Eph 4:12; 2Cor 8:4; 1Tm 1:12; 3:10; Heb 6:10; Rev 2:19*.

> [19]*Therefore, brothers, since we have confidence to enter the Most Holy Place by the blood of Jesus, [20]by a new and living way opened for us through the curtain, that is, his body, [21]and since we have a great priest over the house of God, [22]let us draw near to God with a sincere heart in full assurance of faith, having our hearts sprinkled to cleanse us from a guilty conscience and having our bodies washed with pure water.* **(Heb 10:19-22)**

It is worth mentioning that the etymology of the word we now know as "liturgy" is "the work of the *people*," which is the major connection between its use in the NT and its secular use. Worship is done by all, not just by priests, pastors, or praise teams.

Worship is done by all, not just by priests, pastors, or praise teams.

While *leitourgia*, along with its various forms, is used most often in the context of gathered worship, *diakonia* is more about "doing" ministry, especially in the offices of prophet, elder, or deacon. A basic meaning of the word is "to wait at table." H.W. Beyer comments that it has "the special quality of indicating very personally the service rendered to another" (**81**). This kind of servant is "always one who serves on Christ's behalf and continues Christ's service for the outer and inner man" (**Hess, 544**). The authors of the NT valued both ministering to God and ministering to God's people. Worship is never confined only to Sunday, or only to a building.

Don Saliers contends, "The tensive unity of *leitourgia* and *diakonia* cannot be reduced. Worship of God is both in the assembly of praise and in the

Worship is never confined only to Sunday, or only to a building.

works of mercy" (**189**). Or, as Paul Hoon more pointedly acknowledges, ". . . surely we cannot call any experience of worship authentic which leaves conduct unaffected" (**54**). If people leave the Sunday gathering without being changed and prepared to live as servants of Christ Jesus, something is

If people leave the gathering unchanged and unready to serve, something is missing. missing. A body of believers that is truly worshiping God will be known in the community, not for its style of music, its charismatic preacher, or its magnificent building, but for its consistent, unselfish acts of service.

Revelation—Complete Allegiance

Revelation exhibits worship that is wholeheartedly devoted to the service of God. The saints, who have endured great tribulation and been washed in the blood of the Lamb, *"serve* [latreuo] *him day and night in his temple."* Therefore *"he who sits on the throne will spread his tent"* (or *tabernacle*) *"over them"* (**Rev 7:14-15**).

Marva Dawn encourages: "If we keep remembering how God continues to tent over us, then we can live every moment of our lives in a worshipful way. We will BE Church in the excellence with which we work, in the way we care for those around us, in the way we steward our resources for the sake of the world. If we are encouraged by our gathering together, then we will more eagerly make everything we do worship-full" (*Royal*, 275).

Peterson calls attention to another major theme in Revelation, the distinction between true worship and the worship of idols. "Acceptable worship," he says, "involves acknowledging and accepting God's claim for exclusive devotion and loyalty by rejecting every alternative" (265). The culture at the time of John's writing sets the backdrop for this aspect of worship. Idol worship was everywhere, and citizens were expected to worship emperors as gods. For followers of Christ the choice had to be made, and Revelation reveals the severe consequences for choosing wrongly. Even the angel dismissed worship, insisting that it is for God and God alone:

> [9]*Then the angel said to me, "Write: 'Blessed are those who are invited to the wedding supper of the Lamb!'"* And he added, "These are the true words of God."

> [10]*At this I fell at his feet to worship him. But he said to me, "Do not do it! I am a fellow servant with you and with your brothers who hold to the testimony of Jesus. Worship God! For the testimony of Jesus is the spirit of prophecy."* (**Rev 19:9-10**)

Elsewhere, the dragon and the beast are worshiped, setting up a cosmic struggle. To choose God, is to "recognize Him in all His power and glory as Creator and judge, acknowledge His exclusive sovereign rights and claim upon you (*Rev 14:7*)" (**Schönweiss, 877**).

Revelation portrays continual worship (*proskuneo*) and service (*latreuo*) before the Throne (**Rev 4:10; 7:15; 22:3**). As in the rest of God's Word, the two are not separate entities, but are intricately bound together. Therefore, maintains Robert Lowery, the book is highly relevant to the issue of appropriate worship.

> John is convinced that what people do in their worship lies behind what they do in the world. Worship is not to be limited to a gathering of believers on a certain day of the week; the worship or service to God is to be offered continually. Indeed, John's notion fits in with Paul's notion that Christians are to present their lives daily to God in complete surrender to his will (*Rom 12:1*). It's a complete heart surrender. If God is truly acknowledged in all that Christians say and do, the war at the heart of things is won because the war of the heart is won. (**95**).

Servanthood and worship transfer from the OT practices of priestly service, sacrifices, and covenant keeping to the NT relationship to Jesus Christ, who has accomplished all of these things. How then, does our worship reflect this once-and-for-all act of redemption? John Frame elucidates, "Essentially, what is left is worship in the broad sense: A life of obedience to God's word, a sacrifice of ourselves to His purposes. All of life is our priestly service, our homage to the greatness of our covenant Lord" (**30**).

THE INDWELLING SPIRIT

By the time of Paul, the understanding of the temple, and thus the presence of God, has moved from a place (the temple in Jerusalem), to a person (Jesus Christ), to a people (the church). It is the Holy Spirit who makes the latter possible. Gordon Fee expounds, "The church, corporately and individually, is the place of God's personal presence, by the Spirit. This is what marks God's new people off from 'all the other people on the face of the earth'" (*Empowering*, 8).

> **By Paul's time, the understanding of God's presence has moved from a place to a person to a people.**

Paul makes this truth abundantly clear in his letter to the Corinthians:

> [16]*Don't you know that you yourselves are God's temple and that God's Spirit lives in you?* [17]*If anyone destroys God's temple, God will destroy him; for God's temple is sacred, and you are that temple.* (**1Cor 3:16-17**)[9]

"You" in this passage is plural; therefore the admonition is to the body as a whole. The Corinthian church is God's temple via the unifying work of the Holy Spirit. The Corinthians were under scrutiny because of their divisiveness. Paul insists that anyone causing harm to God's temple, which has been made holy, is in grave danger from the hand of God.

"Indwelling" is a major tenet of Paul's teaching concerning the Holy Spirit. For example, he encourages Timothy to *"Guard the good deposit that was entrusted to you—guard it with the help of the Holy Spirit who lives in us"* (**2Tm 1:14**). The verb, *enoikeo*, "to dwell," writes Jack Cottrell, implies "not a temporary, transient visit, but a permanent settling down. When the Spirit enters into us, He 'unpacks His bags,' as it were, and becomes a permanent resident. He moves in and makes Himself at home within us" (**Power, 336**). Apart from the

---

[9] See also **2Cor 6:16; Eph 2:21**.

work of the Holy Spirit we are helpless to fulfill the holiness expected of us because of our relationship to a holy God.

Norman Harrison describes the results of this process:

> This indwelling Spirit, one with our spirit, is more than a presence with us. He is a moulding, transforming power. To the end of Jesus' ministry, taught of Him though they were, His followers, even His intimates, remained unstable, cowardly and undependable: His was but an influence without. When, however, the Spirit was come, these same men became at once the embodiment of fidelity, courage and conviction. True, Jesus had left them, but His Spirit within made them as new men. So does He desire to work in every believer. (**22**)

In his epistles, John emphasizes God's indwelling: *"Those who obey his commands live in him, and he in them. And this is how we know that he lives in us: We know it by the Spirit he gave us"* (*1Jn 3:24*; see also *2:14; 3:9; 4:12*). Keith Warrington describes this indwelling as "more than an awareness of God," indicating that the present tense[10] indicates a continuous relationship between God and the believer (**206**). This consistent, constant, empowering relationship sustains our ability to remain in communion with God and with each other.

> This kind of radical awakening does not occur overnight. It takes time. It is the work of our whole life and is only fully accomplished in eternity. It's the gradual unveiling of what is true, so we are not equipped to move there in just one step. We will move ahead and then back, again and again. It doesn't mean that we give up our preferences, personalities or choices. What is gradually altered is the controlling urgency, the unequivocal and unquestioned preeminence these things have over us. By the power of the Holy Spirit, we choose to live each day leaning into our new life in Christ and practicing this way of being and doing. Such a life is the fruit of the Holy Spirit (**Labberton, 168**).[11]

"By the power of the Holy Spirit, we choose to live each day leaning into our new life in Christ."

---

[10] Of *meno*, "to abide," here translated "live."

[11] See *Gal 5:22-25*.

THE WORK OF THE HOLY SPIRIT IN WORSHIP

The ability of the Spirit to empower and transform is a substantial factor in all manner of worship, personal or corporate. Jesus' allusion to the Holy Spirit in *John 4*, *"Worship the Father in spirit and in truth,"* indicates this, as does Paul's admonition to the Philippians, *"We worship [latreuo] by the Spirit of God"* (*Php 3:3*). We have already seen that His indwelling allows believers to show forth holiness. But this is not the only way that Paul sees the Holy Spirit enabling our worship. For Paul, Fee suggests, "the gathered church was first of all a worshiping community; and the key to their worship was the presence of the Holy Spirit" (*Empowering*, 884). In *Ephesians 5:18-19*, the Spirit gives impetus for singing and making music, as well as giving thanks. The letter to Corinth indicates that the Spirit was expected to be at work in the gathered assembly, and that His work resulted in spontaneous, assorted, and creative acts of worship. He was at work in *every believer*, not just a chosen few (*1Cor 14:26*). Fee makes note that chaos was not permitted, however. "The God whom they worship," he says, "is a God of peace (*v 33*), whose character is to be reflected in both the manner and content of their worship. Therefore, disorder is out" (*Empowering*, 885).

Entering into God's presence cannot be accomplished by human design. It is the Holy Spirit, Paul Waitman Hoon claims, who is the "immanent mode of God's presence." Therefore, "As God present in the aspects of intimacy and power, the Holy Spirit also informs worship with a supernatural energy that at times appears to be irrational. Thus even at considerable risk, Christian thought has never desired to exclude the Holy Spirit in its manifestation as energy but has taken up the position of St. Paul, who while warning the Corinthians against the excesses of the Spirit, nevertheless did not forbid them" (117).

In *John 16:3*, Jesus promises His disciples that after He is no longer on this earth to teach them, the Spirit will be avail-

The Spirit guides in "the deep things of God" through the Word of God, a nonnegotiable aspect of our gatherings.

able to *"guide them into all truth."* Paul tells us that the Holy Spirit guides us in *"the deep things of God"* (*1Cor 2:10*). He does so through the Word of God, which is, as previously noted, a nonnegotiable aspect of corporate gatherings. The Word cannot, however, be relegated only to Sunday, but should be an integral part of every believer's life.

While praying should be indispensable to both private and corporate worship, many churches have dismissed it as an integral part of corporate worship. It seems that the

The gathered Body of Christ has lost the art of prayer.

gathered Body of Christ has lost the art of prayer. We should be empowered by the knowledge that the Holy Spirit aids us in our prayers even when we do not know how to pray:

> In the same way, the Spirit helps us in our weakness. We do not know what we ought to pray for, but the Spirit himself intercedes for us with groans that words cannot express. And he who searches our hearts knows the mind of the Spirit, because the Spirit intercedes for the saints in accordance with God's will. (*Rom 8:26*)

Another aspect of corporate worship that relies upon the Holy Spirit is fellowship (*koinonia*), seen in Acts at the heart of Christian gatherings. Paul portrays the Church as one body, both unified and gifted by the Spirit (*Eph 4:3-16; 1Cor 12:12-26*). Yet the saints at Corinth drew harsh words from Paul because they were divided in their giftedness. The gifts were of little use if the Corinthians were not relying on the Spirit to use them for the good of the Body. *"Now to each one the manifestation of the Spirit is given for the common good"* (*1Cor 12:7*). Cottrell admonishes, "The Spirit gives ministries and abilities to individuals, so that those individuals may use these gifts to meet the needs of God's covenant people as a whole" (*Power*, 395). Perhaps the church today would do well to look beyond oratory and musical skills to find Spirit-given abilities that could minister to the community in hundreds of different ways.

Unity at the Table is made possible through the work of the Holy Spirit.

> [16]Is not the cup of thanksgiving for which we give thanks a participation in the blood of Christ? And is not the bread that we break a participation in the body of Christ? [17]Because there is one loaf, we, who are many, are one body, for we all partake of the one loaf. (*1Cor 10:16-17*)

The word translated "participation" in this passage is *koinonia*. As our fellowship with each other must be empowered by the Holy Spirit, so must our fellowship with Jesus Christ (see ch. 2). Koenig emphasizes that

> because of the Spirit's intensive presence at the eucharistic celebration, we are able—if open to that presence—to see ourselves with the loving eyes of God, and our neighbors as ourselves. As a result, we can then offer ourselves up for God's mission, along with our neighbors at the Lord's table, who are engaged in the same process of discernment. (**229**)

THE CONNECTION BETWEEN PUBLIC AND PRIVATE WORSHIP

One problem we face in our corporate gatherings today is the disconnectedness between public and private worship. It seems that many attend gatherings Sunday after Sunday, expecting some elusive experience to one day rise up and connect them to God. But when they leave the building, they leave God behind, and their lives during the week have no relationship to the praising, listening, praying, and giving that may have taken place inside the sacred walls.

Our study should lead us to the conclusion that worship as a lifestyle and worship in the assembly are inseparable.

Worship as a lifestyle and worship in the assembly are inseparable. The various acts that occur during our community gatherings serve a twofold purpose. They are, in and of themselves, our unselfish offerings to God. We do not get to pick them according to our fleshly desires, but gladly pray, sing, listen, give, and serve in whatever manner is made available to us. We defer to one another, believing that the Holy Spirit gifts us in whatever way He sees fit. We are filled with joy at the prospect of the presence of the Holy One in our midst. We remember actively, not passively, the life, death, and resurrection of our Lord Jesus Christ as we partake of His Holy Meal.

CONCLUSION

All of these actions, while themselves being worship, miraculously form our hearts, souls, and minds. We are fed by the Word to learn greater truths about God. We are empowered by singing to praise God every day in our ordinary lives. We are encouraged by one another to live worthy of our calling. We mutually approach God's throne and are promised that He will hear us. We eat of His body and drink of His blood, and know that the once-and-for-all work of Christ has bought our salvation. We are reminded that we have the power of the Holy Spirit to light our darkened paths and strengthen our weary hearts. *We can hardly wait to leave, to be light in the world, yet we can hardly wait to come back to praise God all over again.*

What Do You Say?

1. How do you think most Christians view the relationship between Sunday gatherings and personal worship? Do we generally come prepared for corporate worship?

2. Since service and worship are so closely related, how might they be connected in our corporate gatherings in a practical way?

3. Do you think the importance of the Holy Spirit in worship has been overemphasized or underemphasized in your context?

CONCLUSION

The Ancient Israelites were formed and informed by their acts of worship. As they offered prayers, sacrifices and other offerings before God, they recognized His power to intervene in their daily lives. For them, He was Creator, Redeemer, Covenant Maker, Savior, and Master. They knew that He was looking at their hearts and that worship activities were meaningless apart from sincerity and acts of service. Yet they continued their corporate gatherings, which had been commanded. The great story of redemption was at the center.

The earliest Christians were formed and informed by their acts of worship. As they participated in teaching and preaching, prayers, fellowship, baptisms, and the Lord's Supper, they recognized His power to intervene in their daily lives. For them, He was Creator, Redeemer, Covenant Maker, Savior, and Master. They had seen, eaten with, and been taught by the Incarnate Word. *"Worship in spirit and truth,"* He had said. *"I am with you always, to the very end of the age,"* He had promised. *"Go and make disciples,"* He had commanded. They were empowered by His Spirit. They knew that He was looking at their hearts, and that worship activities were meaningless apart from sincerity and acts of service. Yet they continued their corporate gatherings, as was commanded. The great story of salvation was at the center.

God Almighty, Maker of heaven and earth, and His Son, the Lamb who was slain, are now seated in the great throne room of heaven. Together with the Spirit, they are Creator, Redeemer, Covenant Maker, Savior, and Master. There they acknowledge the saints of the past and present, while worship surrounds them day and night. They await the day when the final battle is won. The outcome is certain. And we, the created, the redeemed, the covenant keepers, the saved, the servants, will gather there, and finally understand worship. Hallelujah!

EPILOGUE

My youngest nephew is a lovey-dovey child. This is not a Frankland trait—he has clearly inherited it from his mother. For many of his early years, he would say "I love you" to complete strangers: waitresses and waiters, workers at amusement parks, checkers at the grocery store. When he was about three years old, we were out on the patio and he saw across the way a girl playing on the playground. "She is all alone," he said. "Yes, she is," I acknowledged. "I want to be with her," his sweet little heart declared. He was, and still is, a favorite of his teachers, who have been beguiled by his charm.

But my favorite act of love was a word accompanied by a gesture. He would find someone sitting comfortably in a chair, stand in front of them, hold up his little arms, and say "lap."

Worship is too big for us. But God accepts our meager attempts when they are accompanied by obedience and sacrifice. May you find, in your journey of worship, a place in His loving embrace.

WHAT OTHER AUTHORS SAY

Ashby, Godfrey. *Go Out and Meet God: A Commentary on the Book of Exodus*. Grand Rapids: Eerdmans, 1998.

Averbeck, Richard E. "Worshiping God in Spirit." In *Authentic Worship*, pp. 107-133. Ed. by Herbert W. Bateman IV. Grand Rapids: Kregel, 2002.

Baer, D.A., and R.P. Gordon. *"hesed."* In vol. 2, *New International Dictionary of Old Testament Theology & Exegesis*. Ed. by Willem A. VanGemeren. Grand Rapids: Zondervan, 1997.

Baird, William. *The Corinthian Church—A Biblical Approach to Urban Culture*. Nashville: Abingdon, 1964.

Balentine, Samuel E. *The Torah's Vision of Worship*. Minneapolis: Fortress Press, 1999.

Balz, Horst. *"latreuo."* In vol. 2, *Exegetical Dictionary of the New Testament*. Ed. by Horst Balz & Gerald Schneider. Grand Rapids: Eerdmans, 1981.

Beachy, Alvin. *Worship as Celebration of Covenant and Incarnation*. Newton, KS: Faith and Life Press; Scottdale, PA, 1968.

Berglund, Brad. *Reinventing Sunday*. Valley Forge, PA: Judson Press, 2001.

Beyer, H.W. *"diakoneo"* (etc.). In vol. 2, *Theological Dictionary of the New Testament*. Ed. by Gerhard Kittel. Trans. by Geoffrey W. Bromiley. Grand Rapids: Eerdmans, 1964.

Binz, Stephen J. *The God of Freedom and Life: A Commentary on the Book of Exodus*. Collegeville, MN: The Liturgical Press, 1993.

Birch, Bruce, et al. *A Theological Introduction to the Old Testament*. 2nd ed. Nashville: Abingdon, 2005.

Blackman, E.C. "Incarnation." In vol.3, *The New Interpreter's Dictionary of the Bible*. Ed. by George Buttrick. Nashville: Abingdon, 1962.

Blowers, Paul M. "Creeds and Confessions." In *The Encyclopedia of the Stone Campbell Movement*, pp. 252-256. Ed. by Douglas A. Foster. Grand Rapids: Eerdmans, 2004.

Bonhoeffer, Dietrich. *Life Together*. New York: Harper & Row, 1954.

Borchert, Gerald L. *John 1–11*. The New American Commentary. Vol. 25A. Ed. by E. Ray Clendenen. Nashville: Broadman and Holman, 1996.

Bromiley, Geoffrey W. "Elements of New Testament Worship." In *The Complete Library of Christian Worship*, Vol. One, pp. 106-110. Ed. by Robert E. Webber. Nashville: Star Song, 1994.

Bruce, F.F. *Commentary on the Book of the Acts*. Grand Rapids: Eerdmans, 1974.

Brueggemann, Walter. *A Commentary on **Jeremiah**: Exile and Homecoming*. Grand Rapids: Eerdmans, 1998.

_____. "**Exodus**." In *The New Interpreter's Bible: A Commentary in Twelve Volumes*. Vol. 1, pp. 675-981. Ed. by Leander E. Keck et al. Nashville: Abingdon, 1994.

_____. *Isaiah 1–39*. Louisville, KY: John Knox Press, 1998.

_____. *Worship in **Ancient** Israel: An Essential Guide*. Nashville: Abingdon, 2005.

Bultmann, Rudolf. "*alētheia*." In *Theological Dictionary of the New Testament: Abridged in One Volume*. Ed. by Gerhard Kittel and Gerhard Friedrich. Trans. by Geoffrey W. Bromiley. Grand Rapids: Eerdmans, 1985.

Campbell, Alexander. *The Christian System*. Cincinnati: Standard Publishing, 1901.

_____. "A Restoration of the Ancient Order of Things. No. 6. On the Breaking of Bread. No. I." *The Christian Baptist* 3 (1825): 13.

Carson, D.A. "Worship under the Word." In *Worship by the Book*, pp. 11-63. Ed. by D.A. Carson. Grand Rapids: Zondervan, 2002.

Chafin, Kenneth L. *The Communicator's Commentary: 1,2 Corinthians*. Ed. by Lloyd J. Ogilvie. Waco, TX: Word Books, 1985.

Chalmers, Thomas. Quoted in C.H. Spurgeon. *The Treasury of David: An Expository and Devotional Commentary on the Psalms. Psalms 1–89. Vol. 2, Psalms 27–52*. 1882–1887. Grand Rapids: Baker, reprint, 1984.

Chambers, Oswald. *My Utmost for His Highest*. Grand Rapids: Discovery House, 1989.

Charnock, Stephen. *Discourses upon the Existence and Attributes of God*. London: H.G. Bohn, 1853.

Clapp, Rodney. *A Peculiar People*. Downers Grove, IL: InterVarsity, 1996.

Cottrell, Jack. *Power from On High: What the Bible Says about the Holy Spirit*. Joplin, MO: College Press, 2007.

_____. *Romans*. The College Press NIV Commentary. 2 vols. Joplin, MO: College Press, 1996, 1998.

Crichton, J.D. "A Theology of Worship." In *The Study of Liturgy*, pp. 3-31. Rev. ed. Ed. by Cheslyn Jones et al. New York: Oxford University Press, 1992.

Cullman, Oscar. "The Breaking of Bread." In *The Complete Library of Christian Worship*. Vol. 1, pp. 318-319. Ed. by Robert E. Webber. Nashville: Star Song, 1994.

Davidson, Robert. *The Vitality of Worship: A Commentary on the Book of Psalms*. Grand Rapids: Eerdmans, 1998.

Dawn, Marva. *Reaching Out without Dumbing Down*. Grand Rapids: Eerdmans, 1995.

_____. *A Royal 'Waste' of Time*. Grand Rapids: Eerdmans, 1999.

Delitzsch, Franz. *Biblical Commentary on the Psalms*. Vol. 2. Trans. by Francis Bolton. Grand Rapids: Eerdmans, 1949.

Dodd, C.H. *The Apostolic Preaching and Its Developments*. New York: Harper, 1960.

_____. *The Interpretation of the Fourth Gospel*. Cambridge: University Press, 1953.

Dumbrell, William J. *The End of the Beginning: Revelation 21–22 and the Old Testament*. Grand Rapids: Baker Book House, 1985.

Edersheim, Alfred. *The Temple: Its Ministry and Services*. Peabody, MA: Hendrickson, 1994.

Fee, Gordon D. *God's Empowering Presence: The Holy Spirit in the Letters of Paul*. Peabody, MA: Hendrickson, 1994.

_____. "History as Context for Interpretation." In *The Act of Bible Reading*, pp. 10-32. Ed. by Elmer Dyk. Downers Grove, IL: InterVarsity, 1996.

Fergusson, David A.S. *The Cosmos and the Creator*. London: SPCK, 1998.

Fernando, Ajith. *The NIV Application Commentary: Acts*. Ed. by Terry Muck. Grand Rapids: Zondervan, 1998.

Foster, Richard. *Celebration of Discipline*. New York: Harper and Row, 1978.

Frame, John M. *Worship in Spirit and Truth*. Phillipsburg, NJ: P & R Publishing, 1996.

Gorman, Frank H. Jr. *Divine Presence and Community: A Commentary on the Book of Leviticus*. Grand Rapids: Eerdmans, 1997.

Greet, Brian A. *Broken Bread in a Broken World*. Valley Forge, PA: Judson Press, 1970.

Greevaen, Heinrich. "*proskuneo*." In vol. 6, *Theological Dictionary of the New Testament*, Ed. by Gerhard Friedrich.

Trans. by Geoffrey W. Bromiley. Grand Rapids: Eerdmans, 1968.

Grenz, Stanley J., and Roger E. Olson. *20th Century Theology: God and the World in a Transitional Age.* Downers Grove, IL: InterVarsity, 1992.

Gunkel, Hermann. *The Psalms: A Form-Critical Introduction.* Trans. by Thomas M. Horner. Philadelphia: Fortress, 1967.

Guthrie, Donald. *New Testament Theology.* Downers Grove, IL: InterVarsity, 1973.

Hall, Gary. *Deuteronomy.* The College Press NIV Commentary. Joplin, MO: College Press, 2000.

Harrison, Norman B. *His Indwelling Presence.* Chicago: The Bible Institute Colportage Association, 1928.

Hauck, Friedrich. *"koinos"* (etc). In vol. 3, *Theological Dictionary of the New Testament,* Ed. by Gerhard Kittel. Trans. by Geoffrey W. Bromiley. Grand Rapids: Eerdmans, 1965.

Hawthorne, Gerald F. "The Lord's Supper." In *The Complete Library of Christian Worship.* Vol. 1, pp. 319-325. Ed. by Robert E. Webber. Nashville: Star Song, 1994.

Hendrickson, William. *More Than Conquerors: An Interpretation of the Book of Revelation.* Grand Rapids: Baker Books, 1939, 1967.

Herbert, A.S. *Worship in Ancient Israel.* Richmond, VA: John Knox Press, 1959.

Hess, Klaus. "Serve, Deacon, Worship." In vol. 3, *The New International Dictionary of New Testament Theology,* pp. 544-553. Ed. by Colin Brown. Grand Rapids: Zondervan, 1978.

Hieronymus, Lynn. *What the Bible Says about Worship.* Joplin, MO: College Press, 1984.

Hill, Andrew E. *Enter His Courts with Praise!* Grand Rapids: Baker Books, 1993.

Hoon, Paul Whitman. *The Integrity of Worship.* Nashville: Abingdon, 1971.

Hurtado, Larry W. *At the Origins of Christian Worship.* Grand Rapids: Eerdmans, 1999.

Idelsohn, A.Z. *Jewish Liturgy and Its Development.* New York: Sacred Music Press, 1932.

Janzen, J. Gerald. *Exodus.* Louisville, KY: Westminster John Knox Press, 1997.

Kittel, Gerhard. *"logikos."* In vol. 4, *Theological Dictionary of the New Testament.* Ed. by Gerhard Kittel. Trans. by Geoffrey W. Bromiley. Grand Rapids: Eerdmans, 1964.

Koenig, John. *The Feast of the World's Redemption.* Harrisburg, PA: Trinity Press International, 2000.

Labberton, Mark. *The Dangerous Act of Worship.* Downers Grove, IL: InterVarsity, 2007.

Lambert, Bryon C. *The Restoration of the Lord's Supper and the Sacramental Principle.* Los Angeles: Westwood Christian Foundation, 1992.

Laney, J. Carl, and John W. Schmitt. *Messiah's Coming Temple.* Grand Rapids: Kregel, 1997.

Larsson, Göran. *Bound for Freedom: The Book of Exodus in Jewish and Christian Traditions.* Peabody, MA: Hendrickson, 1999.

Leonard, Janice E. "The **Concept** of Covenant in Biblical Worship." In *The Complete Library of Christian Worship.* Vol. 1, pp. 56-65. Ed. by Robert Webber. Nashville: StarSong, 1993.

_____. *I Will Be Their God: Understanding the Covenant.* Chicago: Laudemont Press, 1992.

_____. "The **Tabernacle** of David." In *The Complete Library of Christian Worship.* Vol. 1, pp. 120-123. Ed. by Robert Webber. Nashville: Star Song, 1993.

Leonard, Richard C. "Old Testament **Vocabulary** of Worship." In *The Complete Library of Christian Worship.*

Vol. 1, p. 3-9. Ed. by Robert Webber. Nashville: StarSong, 1993.

_____. "**Prophetic** Leadership in Old Testament Worship." In *The Complete Library of Christian Worship.* Vol. 1, pp. 164-166. Ed. by Robert Webber. Nashville: Star Song, 1993.

_____. "**Service** of the Word." In *The Complete Library of Christian Worship.* Vol. 1, pp. 294-306. Ed. by Robert Webber. Nashville: StarSong, 1993.

Liefield, Walter L. *The NIV Application Commentary: 1 & 2 Timothy/Titus.* Grand Rapids: Zondervan, 1999.

Liesch, Barry. *People in the Presence of God.* Grand Rapids: Zondervan, 1988.

Longman, Tremper III. *Immanuel in Our Place.* Phillipsburg, NJ: P&R Publishing, 2001.

_____. "**Lament**." In *Cracking Old Testament Codes*, pp. 197-215. Ed. by D. Brent Sandy and Ronald L. Giese Jr. Nashville: Broadman & Holman, 1995.

Lowery, Robert A. *Revelation's Rhapsody: Listening to the Lyrics of the Lamb.* Joplin, MO: College Press, 2006.

Manahan, Ronald E. "The Worshiper's Approach to God: An Exposition of Psalm 15." In *Authentic Worship*, pp. 55-77. Ed. by Herbert W. Bateman IV. Grand Rapids: Kregel, 2002.

Martin, Ralph. *Worship in the Early Church.* London: Marshall, Morgan and Scott, 1974.

_____. "Worship in the **Patriarchal** Period." In *The Complete Library of Christian Worship.* Vol. 1, p. 95. Ed. by Robert Webber. Nashville: Star Song, 1993.

McCann, J. Clinton Jr. "The **Book** of Psalms." In *The New Interpreter's Bible.* Vol. 4, pp. 641-1280. Nashville: Abingdon, 1996.

_____. *A Theological Introduction to the Book of Psalms.* Nashville: Abingdon, 1993.

Meyer, Stephen G. "Neuropsychology and Worship." *Journal of Psychology and Theology* 3 (1975): 281-289.

Moore, Mark. *The Chronological Life of Christ.* Vol. 2. Joplin, MO: College Press, 1996.

Mowinckel, Sigmund. *The Psalms in Israel's Worship.* Trans. by D.R. Ap-Thomas. Grand Rapids: Eerdmans, 2004.

Muilenburg, James. *The Way of Israel: Biblical Faith and Ethics.* London: Routledge & Kegan Paul, 1962.

Nixon, R.E. "Glory." In *New Bible Dictionary,* 3rd ed. Ed. by J.D. Douglas et al. Downers Grove, IL: InterVarsity, 1996.

O'Brien, Peter T. *The Epistle to the Philippians: A Commentary on the Greek Text.* Grand Rapids: Eerdmans, 1991.

Owens, Ron. *Return to Worship.* Nashville: Broadman & Holman, 1999.

Paige, Terrence P. "Holy Spirit." In *Dictionary of Paul and His Letters,* pp. 404-413. Ed. by Gerald F. Hawthorne and Ralph P. Martin. Downers Grove, IL: InterVarsity, 1993.

Paris, Andrew. *What the Bible Says about the Lord's Supper.* Joplin, MO: College Press, 1986.

Peterson, David. *Engaging with God.* Grand Rapids: Eerdmans, 1992.

Pfatteicher, Philip H. *Liturgical Spirituality.* Harrisburg, PA: Trinity Press International, 1997.

Pink, Arthur W. *Gleanings in Exodus.* Chicago: Moody Press, n.d.

Ralston, Timothy J. "Scripture in Worship: An Indispensable Symbol of Covenant." In *Authentic Worship,* pp. 195-222. Ed. by Herbert W. Bateman IV. Grand Rapids: Kregel, 2002.

Rankin, O.S. "The Extent of the Influence of the Synagogue Service upon Christian Worship." In *Studies in Early Christianity.* 18 Volumes. Vol. 6, *Early Christianity and*

Judasim, pp. 173-178. Ed. by Everett Ferguson. New York: Garland Publishing, 1933.

Read, Ken. *Created to Worship*. Joplin, MO: College Press, 2002.

Richardson, Kurt A. *James*. The New American Commentary. Ed. by E. Ray Clendenen et. al. Nashville: Broadman & Holman, 1997.

Robinson, William. "The Nature and Character of Christian Sacramental Theory and Practice." *Shane Quarterly* 2 (1941): 399-408. Quoted in Charles R. Gresham and Tom Lawson. *The Lord's Supper: Historical Writings on Its Meaning to the Body of Christ*, pp. 213-223. Joplin, MO: College Press, 1993.

Rogers, Adrian. *The Power of His Presence*. Wheaton, IL: Crossway Books, 1995.

Rowley, H.H. *Worship in Ancient Israel: Its Form and Meaning*. Philadelphia: Fortress Press, 1967.

Saliers, Don E. *Worship as Theology: Foretaste of Glory Divine*. Nashville: Abingdon, 1994.

Sampley, J. Paul. "I Corinthians." In *The New Interpreter's Bible: A Commentary in Twelve Volumes*. Vol. 10, pp. 773-1003. Ed. by Leander E. Keck. Nashville: Abingdon, 1994.

Schmemann, Alexander. *Introduction to Liturgical Theology*. Crestwood, NY: St. Vladimir's Seminary Press, 2003.

Schönweiss, Hans, G.T.D. Angel, and Colin Brown. "Prayer." In vol. 2, *The New International Dictionary of New Testament Theology*, pp. 885-886. Ed. by Colin Brown. Grand Rapids: Zondervan, 1978.

Scott, Mark. "**Worship** in Spirit and Truth." Speech delivered to the Association of Christian College Music Educators, Joplin, MO, September 2002.

Senn, Frank C. *Christian Liturgy: Catholic and Evangelical*. Minneapolis: Fortress Press, 1997.

Smalley, Stephen S. *1,2,3 John*. World Biblical Commentary. Vol. 51. Waco, TX: Word, 1984.

Spurgeon, C.H. *The Treasury of David: An Expository and Devotional Commentary on the Psalms. Psalms 1–89.* Vol. 1, *Psalms 1–26.* 1882–1887. Grand Rapids: Baker Book House, reprint, 1984.

Stookey, Laurence Hull. *Eucharist: Christ's Feast with the Church.* Nashville: Abingdon, 1993.

Stott, John R.W. *Between Two Worlds: The Art of Preaching in the Twentieth Century.* Grand Rapids: Eerdmans, 1982.

Thiselton, A.C. "Truth." In *The New International Dictionary of New Testament Theology.* Vol. 1, pp. 874-902. Ed. by Colin Brown with additions and revisions from the German *Theologishes Begriffslexikon zum Neuen Testament.* Ed. by Lothar Coenen et al. Grand Rapids: Zondervan, 1986.

Torrance, J.B. "Confession." In *The New Bible Dictionary*, 3rd ed., pp. 219-220. Ed by D.R.W. Wood. Downers Grove, IL: InterVarsity, 1996.

Travers, Michael E. *Encountering God in the Psalms.* Grand Rapids: Kregel, 2003.

Underhill, Evelyn. *Worship.* New York: Harper & Brothers, 1936.

Wall, Robert W. "The Acts of the Apostles." In *The New Interpreter's Bible: A Commentary in Twelve Volumes*, Vol. 10, pp. 1-391. Ed. by Leander E. Keck et al. Nashville: Abingdon, 1994.

Walvoord, John F., and Roy B. Zuck, eds. *The Bible Knowledge Commentary: An Exposition of the Scriptures.* Wheaton, IL: Victor Books, 1983.

Warrington, Keith. *Discovering the Holy Spirit in the New Testament.* Peabody, MA: Hendrickson, 2005.

Webber, Robert E. "**Features** of Temple Worship." In *The Complete Library of Christian Worship.* Vol. 1, p. 129. Ed. by Robert Webber. Nashville: Star Song, 1993.

_____. "The **History** of Sacraments, Ordinances, and Sacred Actions." In *The Complete Library of Christian*

What Other Authors Say   Works Cited

Worship Vol. 6, p. 79. Ed. by Robert Webber. Nashville: Star Song, 1993.

_____. *Worship,* **Old and New**. Rev.ed. Grand Rapids: Zondervan, 1994.

Wilkinson, David. *The Message of Creation.* Downers Grove, IL: InterVarsity, 2002.

Williams, Donald L. "Biblical Worship as Re-Presentation of Saving Events." In *The Complete Library of Christian Worship.* Vol. 1, pp. 85-91. Ed. by Robert Webber. Nashville: StarSong, 1993.

Witherington, Ben III. *Making a Meal of It: Rethinking the Theology of the Lord's Supper.* Waco, TX: Baylor University Press, 2007.

Witvliet, John D. *Worship Seeking Understanding: Windows into Christian Practice.* Grand Rapids: Baker Academic, 2003.

Young, Edward J. *The Book of Isaiah, Vol. 3.* Grand Rapids: Eerdmans, 1972.

Zorn, Walter. *Psalms.* The College Press NIV Commentary. 2 vols. Joplin MO: College Press, 2004.

Scripture Index

Scripture Index

189

Subject Index